Cambridge Elements

Elements on Women in the History of Philosophy
edited by
Jacqueline P
Monash U

IM YUNJIDANG

Sungmoon Kim
City University of Hong Kong

CAMBRIDGE
UNIVERSITY PRESS

CAMBRIDGE
UNIVERSITY PRESS

University Printing House, Cambridge CB2 8BS, United Kingdom

One Liberty Plaza, 20th Floor, New York, NY 10006, USA

477 Williamstown Road, Port Melbourne, VIC 3207, Australia

314–321, 3rd Floor, Plot 3, Splendor Forum, Jasola District Centre,
New Delhi – 110025, India

103 Penang Road, #05–06/07, Visioncrest Commercial, Singapore 238467

Cambridge University Press is part of the University of Cambridge.

It furthers the University's mission by disseminating knowledge in the pursuit of
education, learning, and research at the highest international levels of excellence.

www.cambridge.org
Information on this title: www.cambridge.org/9781009010665
DOI: 10.1017/9781009024068

First published 2022

A catalogue record for this publication is available from the British Library.

ISBN 978-1-009-01066-5 Paperback
ISSN 2634-4645 (online)
ISSN 2634-4637 (print)

Im Yunjidang

Elements on Women in the History of Philosophy

DOI: 10.1017/9781009024068
First published online: July 2022

Sungmoon Kim
City University of Hong Kong

Author for correspondence: Sungmoon Kim, sungmkim@cityu.edu.hk

Abstract: This Element aims to critically examine the philosophical thought of Im Yunjidang (任允摯堂, 1721–93), a female Korean Neo-Confucian philosopher from the Chosŏn (朝鮮) dynasty (1392–1910), and to present her as a feminist thinker. Unlike most Korean women of her time, Yunjidang had the exceptional opportunity to be introduced to a major philosophical debate among Korean Neo-Confucians, which was focused on two core questions – whether sages and commoners share the same heart–mind and whether the natures of human beings and animals are identical. In the course of engaging in this debate, she was able to reformulate Neo-Confucian metaphysics and the ethics of moral self-cultivation, culminating in her bold ideas of the moral equality between men and women and the possibility of female sagehood. By proposing a "stage approach" to feminism that is also sensitive to the cultural context, this Element shows that Yunjidang's philosophical thought could be best captured in terms of Confucian feminism.

Keywords: Im Yunjidang, Neo-Confucianism, Korean philosophy, Female sagehood, Confucian feminism

ISBNs: 9781009010665 (PB), 9781009024068 (OC)
ISSNs: 2634-4645 (online), 2634-4637 (print)

Contents

Introduction

Confucianism is commonly understood as a universal philosophy. When Confucius transvaluated *ren* (仁) from manliness into the inner virtue that makes a person humane or benevolent and elevated it as the moral virtue par excellence that encompasses the key attributes of all other virtues, he clearly presented Confucian self-cultivation as an ethical program that is available to all human beings.[1] Despite their contrasting accounts of human nature, Mencius and Xunzi, the two most important classical Confucian masters after the demise of Confucius, further articulated the Confucian ethic of moral self-cultivation under the guiding assumption that *anyone* who has successfully undergone the arduous process of moral development can become a sage, the paragon of immaculate moral character. Mencius in particular advanced the idea, which must have been perceived as quite radical by his contemporaries, that all human beings are originally good in the sense that they are born with the "sprouts" (*duan* 端) of cardinal moral virtues – such as *ren*, *yi* (義, righteousness), *li** (禮, ritual propriety), and *zhi* (智, wisdom or, more accurately, the ability to tell right from wrong) – which incline one to become good.[2] Most tellingly, Mencius called human nature "Heaven-decreed,"[3] where Heaven (*tian* 天) was understood by the ancient Chinese as the divine repository of goodness, thereby making it possible that *anyone* dedicated to the Way could carry out the moral mission to make society better and government humane. Therefore, as far as pre-Qin classical Confucianism is concerned, it would not be far-fetched to say that Confucianism aspires to the universal ethics of moral self-cultivation.

What is surprising is that there is little information about how this otherwise universal philosophy was understood, evaluated, or practiced by women, not only during the time of Confucius and his disciples but also after Confucianism became the state ideology and the dominant intellectual tradition throughout the subsequent imperial periods. As H. G. Creel aptly calls him, Confucius might have been one of the first "private teachers" in China who accepted *anyone* as his student as long as the prospect showed him due respect and was eager to learn, regardless of his social and economic

---

[1] For the pre-Confucian meaning of *ren* as "manliness," see E. Bruce Brooks and A. Taeko Brooks, *The Original Analects: Sayings of Confucius and His Successors* (New York: Columbia University Press, 1998), p. 15. On *ren* as the Confucian moral virtue par excellence, see Wing-tsit Chan, "The Evolution of the Confucian Concept of *Jen*," *Philosophy East and West* 4:4 (1955), pp. 295–319; Benjamin I. Schwartz, *The World of Thought in Ancient China* (Cambridge, MA: Belknap, 1985), pp. 75–85.

[2] *Mencius* 2A6. Throughout this Element, I have consulted *Mencius*, trans. D. C. Lau (New York: Penguin, 1970) for the text of the *Mencius*.

[3] *Mencius* 7A1; 7B24.

background.[4] Of his many followers, however, not a single woman is known to have been his student, although there seems to be no textual evidence to suggest that Confucius believed women were incapable of becoming virtuous.[5] None of the interlocutors of Confucius, Mencius, and Xunzi, who (directly or indirectly) helped these progenitors of the Confucian tradition to develop and refine their philosophical ideas, were women. No woman is reported to have made a notable contribution to the rise and subsequent development of Confucianism as a philosophical tradition. In fact, no classical Confucians explicitly criticized the prevailing social conventions that only men participated in public debates and decision-making processes and held public positions. Their admiration of a few extraordinary women of antiquity notwithstanding, none of the classical Confucians seem to have considered women as equal members of the ritual and philosophical communities they created.[6]

The rise of a new mode of Confucianism during the Song dynasty (960–1276) and its predominance as the state ideology and the intellectual trend during the Ming period (1368–1644) changed the political and philosophical landscape of China dramatically. The Song–Ming transformation of Confucianism into so-called Neo-Confucianism, however, which enunciated the Mencian account of good human nature in terms of the universal moral principle called *li* (理), thereby reinforcing the universalist and, arguably, egalitarian dimension of Confucianism, did not bring much change for women. No woman was given an opportunity to be part of the government otherwise undergirded by one of the most meritocratic selection mechanisms in human history,[7] and ritual norms and social conventions continued to prohibit women from presenting their own philosophical reflections on Confucian ethics, politics, and social practices to

---

[4] H. G. Creel, *Confucius and the Chinese Way* (New York: Harper & Row, 1949), p. 29. See also *Analects* 7.7 and 7.8. Throughout this Element, the English translations of the *Analects of Confucius* are adapted, unless noted otherwise, from *The Analects*, trans. D. C. Lau (New York: Penguin, 1979).

[5] Some critics contend that Confucius was a sexist based on the following statement: "Women and servants are particularly hard to manage; if you are too familiar with them, they grow insolent, but if you are too distant they grow resentful" (*Analects* 17.25). Elsewhere in the *Analects*, however, Confucius clearly acknowledges the talent of Tai Ren (太任), the wife of the founder of the Zhou dynasty, King Wen, as vital to the success of the new dynasty (*Analects* 8.20). For careful philological refutations of the charge of Confucius as a sexist, see Paul R. Goldin, "The View of Women in Early Confucianism" and Lisa Raphals, "Gendered Virtue Reconsidered: Notes from the Warring States and Han," both in *The Sage and the Second Sex*, ed. Chenyang Li (Chicago: Open Court, 2000), pp. 139–143 and pp. 225–226, respectively.

[6] On ritual and philosophical communities created by early Confucians (Confucius, in particular), see Robert Eno, *The Confucian Creation of Heaven: Philosophy and the Defense of Ritual Mastery* (Albany: State University of New York Press, 1990).

[7] See Benjamin A. Elman, *Civil Examinations and Meritocracy in Late Imperial China* (Cambridge, MA: Harvard University Press, 2013).

broader intellectual communities. Ironically, until the twentieth century when Confucianism became completely displaced from its dominant political and intellectual position, women had been almost completely excluded from the world of philosophy, making it unthinkable to even imagine a female Confucian philosopher. As a result, almost everything we know about Confucianism as a philosophical and ethical tradition is based on works by male Confucian scholars who, informed by the heavily gendered interpretation of the relationship between *yin* (陰) and *yang* (陽), neither acknowledged moral equality between men and women nor regarded women as equally capable of philosophical thinking and writing.[8] Even in some exceptional cases in which moral equality between men and women was affirmed and promoted in Confucian terms, it was always done by male Confucian scholars whose iconoclastic views deviated from the mainstream Confucian philosophical tradition including Song–Ming Neo-Confucianism.[9]

In this regard, Korea is not dramatically different from China. Confucianism was introduced to the Korean peninsula as early as the fourth century AD, but Confucianism was mainly employed as a political ideology or the method of statecraft until a group of Neo-Confucian scholars founded the Chosŏn dynasty (1392–1910), replacing the Koryŏ (高麗) dynasty (918–1392) that left moral and spiritual matters to Buddhism, which was the state religion. As ardent followers of Song Neo-Confucians, especially the Cheng Brothers (Cheng Hao [程顥, 1032–85] and Cheng Yi [程頤, 1033–1107]) and Zhu Xi (朱熹, 1130–1200), Korean Neo-Confucians struggled to overcome the dualism between Confucian statecraft and Buddhist soulcraft that had characterized the Koryŏ system by embarking on a series of reforms; these culminated in the founding of a new dynasty firmly predicated on a Neo-Confucian moral vision and philosophical doctrine.[10] The defining characteristic of the Chosŏn dynasty, as a Neo-Confucian state, was the rule by scholar-bureaucrats immersed in Confucian classics – the so-called Four Books (*sishu* 四書), in particular, which were canonized by Zhu Xi as essential Neo-Confucian texts. For several centuries that followed, Korean Neo-Confucians transformed both

---

[8] It is debatable whether the *yin–yang* theory is androcentric in nature. But it is generally agreed that Dong Zhongshu (董仲舒, 179–104 BC), one of the most important Confucian philosophers during the early Han period, (re)formulated the relation between *yin* and *yang* in heavily gendered terms. See Robin R. Wang, "Dong Zhongshu's Transformation of '*Yin-Yang*' Theory and Contesting of Gender Identity," *Philosophy East and West* 55:2 (2005), pp. 209–231.

[9] See, for instance, Pauline C. Lee, "Li Zhi and John Stuart Mill: A Confucian Feminist Critique of Liberal Feminism," in *The Sage and the Second Sex*, ed. Li, pp. 113–132.

[10] Kim Yŏng-su (김영수), *Kŏn'gugŭi chŏngch'i: Yŏmal sŏnch'o, hyŏngmyŏnggwa munmyŏng chŏnhwan* (건국의 정치: 여말선초, 혁명과 문명전환) [*The Politics of Founding: Revolution and the Transition of Civilization during the Late Koryŏ and Early Chosŏn Periods*] (Seoul: Ihaksa, 2006).

Chosŏn's state apparatuses and, albeit more slowly, the entire society according to Neo-Confucian philosophical doctrines and ritual theories.[11] By the late seventeenth century, virtually all Koreans belonging to the *yangban* aristocratic class saw themselves as faithful followers of Zhu Xi and any deviation from his Neo-Confucian philosophical doctrines and ritual theories brought the condemnation of the "despoilers of the Way," which signaled the social death of the scholar in question. At worst, it further resulted in the end of the person's life and the discontinuation of his family's lineage.[12]

Not surprisingly, no women were officially involved in the creation and subsequent Neo-Confucian transformation of Chosŏn as Confucian scholars and scholar-officials. Nor were women given the opportunity to receive formal education based on Neo-Confucian classics, let alone to be part of the government by taking (and passing) the civil examination, despite the new state's aspiration to create a truly meritocratic society. As Neo-Confucian social norms became deeply entrenched in every nook and cranny of Korean society, most clearly evidenced in the patrilineal restructuring of the Korean family system,[13] various social and economic entitlements that women had previously enjoyed more or less equally with men were abolished, including the right to inherit the family estate. As a result, women were subject to a rigid patrilineal order in which they existed not so much as free moral agents, but rather as daughters, wives, or mothers, completely severed from the so-called "outer domain" (*wai* 外) or the public space, where they could interact with others through philosophical writings and ritual (and other social) activities and become involved in public affairs by virtue of the intellectual and moral qualities attained through Confucian education and moral self-cultivation. As prescribed by Neo-Confucian ritual norms, in the second half of the Chosŏn dynasty elite Korean women were strictly confined to "the inner chambers" (*nei* 內) within the family. In the inner chambers, most elite women received a limited form of Confucian education specifically tailored for women, mostly based on the texts written by male Confucians in vernacular Korean, whose primary purpose was to help inculcate "female virtues" (k. *yŏdŏk* 女德) or "wifely virtues"

---

[11] Martina Deuchler, *The Confucian Transformation of Korea: A Study of State and Ideology* (Cambridge, MA: Council on East Asian Studies, Harvard University, 1992).

[12] See Martina Deuchler, "Despoilers of the Way – Insulters of the Sages: Controversies over the Classics in Seventeenth-Century Korea," in *Culture and the State in Late Chosŏn Korea*, eds. JaHyun K. Haboush and Martina Deuchler (Cambridge, MA: Harvard University Asia Center, 1999), pp. 91–133.

[13] SoonGu Lee (이순구), "Chosŏnsidae kajok chedoŭi pyŏnhwawa yŏsŏng (조선시대 가족제도의 변화와 여성) [The Change of the Family Structure and Women during the Chosŏn Period]," *Yŏsŏng kojŏn munhak yŏn'gu* 10 (2005), pp. 119–142.

(k. *pudŏk* 婦德) such as submissiveness (*shun* 順), female chastity (*zhen* 貞), and widow suicide (*lie* 烈).[14]

This, however, does not mean that elite women in premodern China and Korea exercised no moral agency at all or took no part in intellectual, artistic, and social activities that helped expand their moral horizons, enlarge their social perspectives, or redefine their selfhood and social identities. As Dorothy Ko powerfully shows, elite Chinese women in seventeenth-century Jiangnan created a distinctive women's culture by forming various literary communities through their poetry, letters, dramas, and literary commentaries. Challenging the conventional image of Chinese women as helpless victims of an oppressive patriarchal social order, Ko calls for a more nuanced understanding of women in premodern China, neither as victims nor free autonomous agents, but as coparticipants of "new womanhood" enabled by wider educational opportunities for women in the most affluent Chinese region at the time and their emergence as writers.[15] While Ko investigates the fascinating rise of new womanhood in Jiangnan China through the formation of a series of literary communities largely outside the mainstream Confucian social order, Patricia Ebrey reconstructs women's social agency in their patriarchal Confucian context, giving special attention to the "opportunities" arising from Song China's otherwise rigidly gendered marriage system and the "choices" women made to shape their own lives; they thus enjoyed considerable autonomy.[16]

Although elite Korean women did not seem to have active interactions among themselves by forming literary communities of the sort that emerged in seventeenth-century Jiangnan China, they, too, though largely confined to inner chambers, engaged in intellectual activities, producing various sorts of literary work such as poetry and literary commentaries.[17] Even the *yangban* ladies who were deeply immersed in Confucian culture did not forfeit their moral agency wholesale. Nor did they become helplessly subject to male domination. Quite the contrary, during the second half of the Chosŏn dynasty many elite Korean women aspired to moral self-cultivation and believed that they could attain sagehood by earnestly fulfilling their female virtues. For example, Lady Chang

---

[14] Martina Deuchler captures the spread of female virtues throughout the Chosŏn dynasty in terms of "indoctrination." See her "Propagating Female Virtues in Chosŏn Korea," in *Women and Confucian Cultures in Premodern China, Korea, and Japan*, eds. Dorothy Ko, JaHyun K. Haboush, and Joan R. Piggott (Berkeley: University of California Press, 2003), pp. 142–169.

[15] Dorothy Ko, *Teachers of the Inner Chambers: Women and Culture in Seventeenth Century China* (Stanford, CA: Stanford University Press, 1994).

[16] Patricia B. Ebrey, *The Inner Quarters: Marriage and the Lives of Chinese Women in the Sung Period* (Berkeley: University of California Press, 1993).

[17] See Yi Hye-sun (이혜순), *Chosŏncho hugi yŏsŏng chisŏngsa* (조선조 후기 여성 지성사) [*The History of Women Intellectuals in Late Chosŏn*] (Seoul: Ihwa yŏja taehakkyo ch'ulp'anbu, 2007).

of Andong (1598–1680), a member of the *yangban* aristocratic class who is best known for her commitment and rigorous practice of Confucian rituals, famously said, "[I]f the action of the sage [consists in] a daily and ordinary morality, it could be a worry that people do not learn the way of sages. If one truly learns of the way of the sages, what difficulty could there be?"[18] Allegedly, Lady Chang immersed herself in the activities pertaining to good motherhood and good wifehood (or daughter-in-law-hood) – namely, the education of children as Confucian gentlemen (*junzi* 君子) and gentlewomen (*nujunji* 女君子) on the one hand, and ancestral rites and reception of guests on the other, the two most important ritual duties for a *yangban* woman. Around two centuries later, Kang Chŏngildang (姜靜一堂, 1772–1832) expressed her unswerving commitment to the ideal of Confucian gentlewoman (and sagehood) in the following poem:

> The way of the sages is like a great road,
> People from past to present have traveled it.
> Learning has no special way to achieve,
> One must explore and search out what is on high.
> The lessons and guidance offered in written records,
> Must be practiced as if before one's eyes.
> Be diligent! Drive straight ahead!
> And together we can roam exquisitely in the realm of the Way![19]

> (聖道如大路,古今之所由. 學問非別致,向上須探求. 卷中指南術, 歷歷在前脩. 勉哉駕直轡, 道域偕優遊.)

As such, we have two different approaches to women's moral agency. The historical studies by Ko and Ebrey approach the question of women's moral agency in the premodern Chinese context from a sociological and anthropological perspective, with a view to understanding the new mode of womanhood emerging from women's participation in literary activities and their formation

---

[18] SoonGu Lee, "The Exemplar Wife: The Life of Lady Chang of Andong in Historical Context," in *Women and Confucianism in Chosŏn Korea: New Perspectives*, eds. Youngmin Kim and Michael J. Pettid (Albany: State University of New York Press, 2011), p. 32. See also Deuchler, "Propagating Female Virtues in Chosŏn Korea," p. 149 for a similar expression by another elite Korean woman.

[19] Kang Chŏngildang (강정일당), *Chŏnildang yugo* 6a (translation assisted by Philip J. Ivanhoe). The page number refers to the digital page of the original classical Chinese text of the *Chŏngildang yugo* (靜一堂遺稿) [*The Bequeathed Writings of Kang Chŏngildang*] available from the Korean Classics database, https://db.itkc.or.kr/dir/item?itemId=MO#/dir/node?dataId=ITKC_MO_1163A_0020_010. For Kang Chŏngildang's idea of Neo-Confucian moral agency and female sagehood, see Sungmoon Kim, "From Wife to Moral Teacher: Kang Chŏngildang on Neo-Confucian Self-Cultivation," *Asian Philosophy* 24:1 (2014), pp. 28–47; and Yi Hye-sun (이혜순), "Kang chŏnildangŭi ye tamnon (강정일당의 예 담론) [Kang Chŏngildang's Discourse of Rituals]," *Ŏmun yŏn'gu* 33 (2005), pp. 135–159.

of literary communities or to identifying the culture-informed "choices" and "opportunities" available to women as social actors. Still, this *external* approach does not critically address how women reflected upon their social existence as prescribed by (Neo-)Confucianism – as daughters, as daughters-in-law, as wives, or as mothers – in reference to the prevailing philosophical concepts and theories of the time. Women's Confucian-prescribed social identities may be bracketed when they venture (momentarily) into the alternative outer world where they could put on a new mantle of womanhood, but when they come back to their inner chambers they are still held by their existing Confucian identities, about which Ko has little to say. Likewise, the fact that women were able to meaningfully control their lives under the Confucian ritual order does not tell us much about how *they* understood moral agency and self-realization in their given social and intellectual context.

In marked contrast, the cases of Lady Chang and Chŏngildang provide an important insight into the inner world of Confucian women, how they understood their own social existence, their ethical life and moral agency, and the intellectual and political worlds in which they found themselves through the philosophical concepts and theories available to them. This is not to argue that examining elite women's positive reappropriation of Confucian moral discourse is the only appropriate way to uncover their moral agency. The point is that an *internal* approach to Confucian women's moral agency cannot be dismissed in favor of an external approach, under the presumption that an internal approach only reveals the social force of dominant Confucian norms in indoctrinating women or that the Confucian moral agency they exercised or the ideal of moral perfection to which they aspired as members of Confucian society was, at best, an expression of their false consciousness. What is needed is a study that investigates Confucian women's self-understanding and their philosophical reflections on themselves, paying full attention to the intellectual, social, and political world that surrounded them. Making a critical distinction between passive indoctrination and constitutive internalization of Confucian values,[20] this alternative approach helps us understand what the universal ethics of Confucian moral self-cultivation meant to women themselves and how it was reinterpreted and reappropriated by those who endeavored to attain sagehood as women. The problem is that there are few (extant) writings by Confucian women that can help us understand their philosophical minds.

This Element aims to embark upon an intellectual journey that has long been considered impossible in the Confucian tradition: to investigate the

---

[20] See also Heisook Kim, "Toward Critical Confucianism: Woman as a Method," *Han'guk yŏsŏng ch'ŏrak* 26 (2016), pp. 131–152.

philosophical thought of a female Confucian philosopher and the contemporary debate on its feminist nature. The philosopher in question is known by her pen name Yunjidang whose family name was Im.[21] In many respects, Im Yunjidang (任允摯堂, 1721–93) was an extraordinary person. First, she was the only female Confucian philosopher throughout the Chosŏn dynasty whose philosophical essays and commentaries on Confucian classics are preserved in their original form.[22] Second, and more importantly, she critically reflected upon some of the key philosophical questions of the time from her unique perspective as a woman. Chŏngildang was one of the later female Korean Confucians who would be profoundly inspired by Yunjidang's bold claim that there should be no difference between men and women in terms of the Heaven-given ability to become a sage.[23] The intellectual lineage that Chŏngildang established between Yunjidang and herself as female Neo-Confucians is unprecedented and it is something that, to my knowledge, had never happened before in China or other Confucian East Asian societies.[24]

This Element consists of three main sections. Section 1 introduces Im Yunjidang's life and the political and intellectual worlds in which she found herself. I pay special attention to the Horak debate, one of the major philosophical debates among Korean Neo-Confucians during the Chosŏn dynasty, and show how Yunjidang's philosophical journey was motivated by some of the key questions raised in this debate. Then, in Section 2, I examine Yunjidang's philosophical thought with a special focus, first, on her metaphysical theory of *li* (理, principle) and *qi* (氣, vital force or, when applied to human beings, psychophysical stuff); second, on her account of human nature (*xing* 性) and heart–mind (*xin* 心); and finally, on her vision of moral equality between men

---

[21] Like most Korean women in the premodern period, Yunjidang's given name is unknown, even though she was a member of the *yangban* aristocratic class.

[22] It is reported that Chŏngildang, too, produced voluminous philosophical writings and commentaries, but most of these were lost due to fire and frequent relocation caused by poverty.

[23] It is important to note, though, that Yunjidang was not the first Neo-Confucian to argue that men and women are morally equal in terms of their Heaven-endowed nature and potential for moral development. Most notably, Yi Sangjŏng (李象靖, 1711–81), one of the (male) leading Neo-Confucian scholars of the T'oegye School, claimed: "Moral principles are rooted in a person's heart; whether they are fully or poorly developed does not depend on being high or low in status, or male or female. Thus, without instruction of books and practice, or without the guidance of teachers and friends, it is not possible to develop innate nature. Loyalty, filiality, righteousness, and chastity can therefore be found in abundance in men, but are rarely heard [to be] in women; they are abundant in the elite, but rarely found in the lower classes. It is not that the [H]eaven-bestowed talents are different. It is alone the circumstances that make them so" (quoted in Deuchler, "Propagating Female Virtues in Chosŏn Korea," p. 148).

[24] See Pak Hyŏn-suk (박현숙), "Kang chŏngildang: Sŏngnihakchŏk namnyŏ p'yŏngdŭngjuŭija (강정일당: 성리학적 남녀평등주의자) [Kang Chŏngildang: A Neo-Confucian Feminist]," *Yŏsŏng munhak yŏn'gu* 11 (2004), pp. 57–79.

and women and the possibility of female sagehood.[25] Finally, in Section 3, I turn to the contemporary debate on Yunjidang: whether she can be understood as a feminist thinker. After critically examining both sides of the debate – the Enthusiasts, on one side, and the Skeptics, on the other, as I call them – I argue that Yunjidang's progressive philosophical thought can be best captured in terms of *Confucian feminism*. In making this argument, I propose what I call a "stage approach" to feminism that is sensitive to the cultural context in which women are situated. This Element concludes by noting some tension between Yunjidang's political conservatism and her progressive feminist philosophy.

1 Yunjidang: The Person and Her World

1.1 The Person

Yunjidang was born into a renowned aristocratic family in 1721.[26] Her great-grandfather was Im Ŭi-paek (任義伯, 1605–67) who served in various important governmental posts during the reigns of King Hyojong (r. 1649–59) and King Hyŏnjong (r. 1659–74), including chief royal secretary, vice-minister of the Bureau of Punishments, and governor of the P'yŏng'an province. He studied Neo-Confucianism under the tutelage of Kim Chang-saeng (金長生, 1548–1631), a former student of Yulgok[27] and one of the most distinguished

---

[25] There is an ongoing debate among contemporary scholars regarding the interpretation of *li* whose literal meaning is (close to) "pattern" – between "principle" and "coherence." Throughout this Element, I generally leave *li*, along with *qi*, untranslated, but where it is translated, I adopt "principle." Elsewhere, I revisited the contemporary debate on *li* in light of the philosophical and political debates between two Korean Neo-Confucians in the wake of the founding of the Chosŏn dynasty. See Sungmoon Kim, "Between Coherence and Principle: *Li* 理 and the Politics of Neo-Confucianism in Late Koryŏ Korea," *Philosophy East and West* 71:2 (2021), pp. 369–392.

[26] For a helpful survey on Yunjidang's life and philosophy, see Kim Kyŏng-mi (김경미), *Im yunjidang p'yŏngjŏn* (임윤지당 평전) [*A Critical Biography of Im Yunjidang*] (Seoul: Han'gyŏrye ch'ulp'an, 2019) and Yi Yŏng-ch'un (이영춘), *Im Yunjidang: Kugyŏk yunjidang yugo* (임윤지당: 국역 윤지당유고) [*Im Yunjidang: A Korean Translation of the Bequeathed Writings of Im Yunjidang*] (Seoul: Hyean, 1998), pp. 13–119. My discussion of Yunjidang's life is deeply indebted to Yi Yŏng-ch'un's seminal study on Yunjidang.

[27] Yulgok refers to Yi I (李珥, 1536–84), one of the two most prominent Korean Neo-Confucians along with Yi Hwang (李滉, 1502–71), also known as T'oegye. Though both T'oegye and Yulgok saw themselves as devoted followers of Zhu Xi, they interpreted Zhu Xi's metaphysics of *li* and *qi* differently, giving rise to two dominant Neo-Confucian scholarly (and political) communities. While T'oegye (and his followers) argued for coissuance of *li* and *qi* (k. *igihobal* 理氣互發), premised on the accounts of *li* and *qi* as two separate entities, Yulgok (and his followers) subscribed to the view that while *qi* issues itself, *li* merely rides on it, which supports the inseparability of *li* and *qi* (k. *kibal isŭng ilto* 氣發理乘一途). After they first seized power in the early seventeenth century, members of the Yulgok school, despite some political fluctuations, maintained both political and intellectual hegemony until the late nineteenth century. On the seminal debate between T'oegye and Yulgok on *li* and *qi*, see Edward Y. J. Chung, *The Korean Neo-Confucianism of Yi T'oegye and Yi Yulgok: A Reappraisal of the "Four-Seven Thesis" and Its Practical Implications for Self-Cultivation* (Albany: State University of New York Press,

Neo-Confucian scholars during the mid Chosŏn period, best known for his original studies on (Neo-)Confucian ritualism. As a member of the Yulgok school, Im Ŭi-paek was also closely acquainted with other leading Neo-Confucians of the time such as Song Siyŏl (宋時烈, 1607–89), arguably the most influential Korean Neo-Confucian of the seventeenth century, and Song Chun-kil (宋浚吉, 1606–72), both leaders of the Yulgok school at the time. Yunjidang's father and grandfather died before passing the civil examination but her eldest brother Im Myŏngju (任命周, 1705–57) held, among other positions, that of inspector at the Office of the Inspector-General, one of the governmental posts most desired by young scholar-bureaucrats as it was commonly believed to be the highway to bureaucratic success. Unfortunately, Im Myŏngju was banished from the government because of his bold criticism of King Yŏngjo (r. 1724–76) and this, in part, caused his untimely death. As Yi Hye-sun powerfully shows, some of Yunjidang's political commentaries seem to have been inspired by her brother's political tribulations and early death.[28]

Of Yunjidang's four other male siblings, two died young, but the remaining two became prominent Neo-Confucian scholars who made significant philosophical contributions to Neo-Confucian metaphysics. Im Sŏngju (任聖周, 1711–88), Yunjidang's second eldest brother, had the biggest influence on her as far as her Neo-Confucian scholarship is concerned. Though Im Sŏngju did not actively pursue an illustrious bureaucratic career, he earned a nationwide reputation as one of the most original thinkers in the history of Korean Neo-Confucianism by developing the monistic theory of *qi* metaphysics in which the importance of *li*, commonly understood in Zhu Xi's Neo-Confucian philosophy as constituting the original nature of human beings and the myriad things in the world, is significantly reduced. Im Sŏngju's philosophy of *qi* was inherited and further developed by his younger brother Im Chŏngju (任靖周, 1727–96; Yunjidang's youngest brother), who like his brother emerged as a prominent Neo-Confucian scholar in the late Chosŏn period. Since Yunjidang's father died when she was only seven-years-old and her eldest brother was employed in the government away from the home, she was educated mainly by Im Sŏngju. He not only taught her basic Confucian ethics and rituals, based on the standard texts for women's education such as the *Xiaoxue* (小學, *The Small Learning*) and the *Lienu zhuan* (列女傳, *The Biographies of the Exemplary Women*), but further introduced her to the world of Neo-Confucian philosophy and classical studies, an extremely rare opportunity for a woman, even for one belonging to

———
1995); and Hyungchan Kim, *Korean Confucianism: The Philosophy and Politics of T'oegye and Yulgok* (London: Rowman & Littlefield International, 2018).

[28] Yi, *Chosŏncho hugi yŏsŏng chisŏngsa*, pp. 127–133.

a prestigious *yangban* family. Throughout Yunjidang's entire life, her brothers were both teachers and philosophical interlocutors, helping her to develop her own philosophical perspectives and ideas.

In his biography of Yunjidang, which he included at the end of the *Yunjidang yugo* (允摯堂遺稿, *The Bequeathed Works of Yunjidang*),[29] Im Chŏngju placed Yunjidang in the mainstream intellectual genealogy of the Yulgok school, which had been the dominant Neo-Confucian school in Korea since the seventeenth century: This ran from Kim Chang-saeng who taught Yunjidang's great-grandfather to Kwŏn Sang-ha (權尙夏, 1641–1721), Song Siyŏl's leading student who taught Yunjidang's father, Im Chŏk (任適, 1685–1728), and from Yi Chae (李縡, 1680–1746), another important scholar of the Yulgok school whose scholarship traces back to Song Siyŏl, to Im Sŏngju, Yunjidang's brother and teacher.[30] Through her family's long scholarly connection with the Yulgok school, Yunjidang was able to participate, albeit indirectly, in the most advanced contemporary philosophical debates of her time. The major debate – commonly known as "the Horak debate" – took place among the students of Song Siyŏl, including those who indirectly influenced the formation of Yunjidang's Neo-Confucian philosophy through her family connections. As will be discussed in Section 2, Yunjidang's development of her own philosophical thought as a woman meant some significant departure from both sides of the debate.

However, Yunjidang's philosophical achievement would not have been possible if she did not have the unusual *freedom* from heavily patriarchal ritual duties that defined the lives of most Korean women from *yangban* families. The irony is that this freedom, which provided Yunjidang with substantial time to engage in classical studies and philosophical inquiry, came with immeasurable personal tragedy.

When Yunjidang was eighteen she married Shin Kwang-yu (申光裕, 1722–47), a man from a *yangban* family of good standing. However, he held no governmental post, and died only eight years into the marriage, leaving no children behind (their only child died in infancy). Following both Chosŏn's law and Neo-Confucian ritual norms that forbade a widow from remarrying, Yunjidang continued to reside in her late husband's household and served his biological and legal mothers until they died, upon which she became the eldest person of the household in her mid-forties.[31] Yunjidang's misfortune did not

---

[29] Note that the *Yunjidang yugo* was coedited by Im Chŏngju and Shin Kwang-u (申光祐, 1726–98), Yunjidang's brother-in-law.

[30] Im Yunjidang (임윤지당), *Yunjidang yugo* (允摯堂遺稿) [*The Bequeathed Writings of Im Yunjidang*], 80a–81a.

[31] Though Yunjidang's husband was the eldest son of Shin Po and his legal wife, he was later adopted by his father's elder brother Shin Kye to succeed the main line of the family lineage. Because of this legal adoption, which was quite common among the *yangban* class in the late

end there. Although she adopted the son of her husband's younger brother (in the same way that her husband had been adopted by his father's elder brother) in order to provide an heir to her husband's descent line, he, too, died at the young age of twenty-seven, six years prior to Yunjidang's death, without having passed the civil service examination, like his (legal) father.[32] Having lost her father, husband, and son (and the unnamed child), Yunjidang was a most unfortunate woman by all measures in late Chosŏn Korean society. Yunjidang lamented, "In retrospect, my life was full of misfortune. Of four ways of being the most destitute (i.e., being without a husband, being without a wife, being old without a child, and being an orphan),[33] I had three and, looking everywhere, I had no one to rely on."[34] On top of all this, most of her siblings died before her, including Im Sŏngju.

Before her mothers-in-law passed away, however, Yunjidang fully dedicated herself to female virtues and the patriarchal social norms on which they rested. According to Shin Kwang-u, Yunjidang studied Confucian classics at night when nobody was around, which made her scholarship largely unknown even to her family members.[35] When she became the oldest member of her (husband's) family with no male members who she was supposed to "follow,"[36] she was practically freed from the patriarchal rituals governing the inner chambers and could finally immerse herself in philosophical studies.

Because Yunjidang gained a reputation posthumously among male Neo-Confucian communities after the publication of the *Yunjidang yugo* as an exemplary Confucian woman who "understood the rites"[37] and since she

---

Chosŏn period as affirmed by Neo-Confucian family rituals, Yunjidang's husband had two mothers – one biological and one legal. On adoption practices during the late Chosŏn period, see Mark A. Peterson, *Korean Adoption and Inheritance: Case Studies in the Creation of Classic Confucian Society* (Ithaca, NY: Cornell University Press, 1996). See also, Deuchler, *Confucian Transformation of Korea*, pp. 48–49.

[32] Yujidang's agonizing sacrificial letter to her adopted son forcefully represents her bitterness in losing him. See *Yunjidang yugo* 60a–62a.

[33] *Mencius* 1B5.

[34] *Yunjidang yugo* 48b. Throughout this Element, all English translations of the *Yunjidang yugo* are mine (unless noted otherwise). I consulted the original Chinese texts digitally remastered at the Korean Classics database, https://db.itkc.or.kr/dir/item?itemId=MO#dir/node? grpId=&itemId=MO&gubun=book&depth=2&cate1=H&cate2=&dataGubun=%EC%84%9C %EC%A7%80&dataId=ITKC_MO_1072A. Page numbers refer to the digital page of the original classical Chinese text.

[35] *Yunjidang yugo* 81b.

[36] According to the moral principle of the "Three Followings for Women" (k. *samchong chi ŭi* 三從 之義), a woman ought to follow her father prior to marriage, her husband, once married, and her son when she becomes a widow.

[37] In the *Lienu zhuan*, Confucius praises a lady named Jing Jiang (敬姜) of the Ji family of Lu, his home country, as one of the virtuous women who "understood the rites." For Confucius's praise of Jing Jiang, see Lisa A. Raphals, "A Woman Who Understood Rites," in *Confucius and the Analects*, ed. Bryan W. Van Norden (New York: Oxford University Press, 2002), pp. 275–302.

never criticized or tried to overcome what contemporary feminists would consider to be deeply gendered roles and virtues, some critics find fault with her as a woman who actively internalized the prevailing patriarchal ritual order and social norms. Some even claim that there is no appreciable difference between Yunjidang's Neo-Confucian philosophy and the philosophical thought developed by Zhu Xi and his Korean (male) followers. In Section 3, I thoroughly examine whether this criticism is warranted. Before making any contemporary judgment on Yunjidang, however, it is imperative to understand both the sociopolitical and intellectual contexts that surrounded Yunjidang, in which she wrestled to establish herself as a philosopher while aspiring to become a sage.

1.2 The World After Ming

Like Chinese Confucian intellectuals who understood themselves as the most civilized (*hua* 華) in the world (*tianxia* 天下) and who regarded those whose lifestyles were not embedded in Confucian rituals and moral norms as "barbarians" (*yi* 夷), Korean Confucians had similarly long considered the Jurchens who resided in the mountainous regions between China and Korea as "barbarians," lacking moral principles such as righteousness and ritual propriety that distinguish humans from nonhuman animals. When the Chosŏn dynasty voluntarily submitted itself to the moral and cultural authority of the Ming – a new Chinese dynasty founded by the Han people – as its foreign vassal state, Korean Neo-Confucians deemed Chosŏn (and themselves) as proud members of the universal civilization maintained by the Chinese emperor venerated as "the Son of Heaven." And this cultural pride led them to believe that their Neo-Confucian state was morally and culturally superior to other non-Chinese peoples including – and especially – the Jurchens. During the formative stage of the Chosŏn dynasty, several military campaigns were launched by the Korean monarchs to "punish" (*zheng* 征 or *tao* 討) the Jurchens who frequently plundered the Koreans living on the northern border; this ended up creating the tributary relationship between Chosŏn and the Jurchens, reminiscent of Chosŏn's own hierarchical relationship with Ming.[38] Still, few Korean Neo-Confucians anticipated the Jurchens' transformation into a "Small China" (*xiao zhonghua* 小中華) like Chosŏn, given their cultural boorishness.[39] For them, the establishment of Chosŏn as

---

Not surprisingly, Confucius's praise made Jing Jiang one of the most honorable names among women in the subsequent development of the Confucian tradition.

[38] In the Confucian political tradition, terms like *zheng* and *tao* are employed to describe a punitive expedition by the higher moral authority against those with a lower moral status.

[39] On the "Small China" ideology of the early Chosŏn Neo-Confucian intellectuals, see Pae Wu-sŏng (배우성), *Chosŏn'gwa chunghwa* (조선과 중화) [*Chosŏn and the Sincocentric Civilization*]

a Neo-Confucian state was a clear testimony to Korea's special standing in the Sinocentric cultural and moral universe.

Korean Neo-Confucians' Sinocentric worldview, predicated on the *hua–yi* distinction, was fundamentally shaken when the Jurchens invaded Chosŏn twice in the seventeenth century, in 1627 and 1636. The Jurchen invasions not only caused the deaths and enslavement of a countless number of Korean people, but, more shockingly, it ultimately made Chosŏn subject to Qing (1636–1912), the dynasty created by the Jurchens after they occupied the Central Plain of China. For Korean Neo-Confucians, the lord–subject relationship between Ming and Chosŏn had been undergirded by the immutable moral principle of righteousness (*yili* 義理) that was also believed to govern the father–son relationship. Thus, the change of moral (and political) allegiance from Ming to Qing meant the collapse of the entire moral universe.[40] When the Chosŏn state and society finally escaped from the devastating aftermath of the wars and restored political order and stability, the first thing that Chosŏn's monarch and the orthodox Neo-Confucian scholar-bureaucrats (i.e., the most passionate followers of Zhu Xi) pursued was to avenge the Ming, understood not so much as the historical state of the Han people but as the moral–cultural center that embodied the Confucian Way, thus bolstering the cosmic order of the moral universe.[41] As Haboush aptly puts it, "While the Ming dynasty reigned in China, the Sino–Korean relation was defined largely in terms of a convergence between the political and the cultural spheres and a harmony between the self and the fellow members of the civilized world."[42]

However, it was not long before mainstream Korean Neo-Confucians realized that using military means to defeat Qing, which was by then firmly consolidated as the new empire of the Son of Heaven, would be an impracticable goal; this realization drove them (followers of Yulgok, now guided by Song Siyŏl) to radically reenvisage the moral standing and cultural identity of Chosŏn from Ming's vassal state into the authentic inheritor of the Confucian Way and

---

(Seoul: Tolbegae, 2014). According to Pae, the early Chosŏn "Small China" ideology took a distinct form in that it was developed with the clear understanding that Korea's local climates and costumes were different from those found in China.

[40] On the moral dilemma faced by the Korean Neo-Confucians between Ming and Qing, see Sungmoon Kim, "Making Peace with the Barbarians: Neo-Confucianism and the Pro-Peace Argument in 17th-Century Korea," *European Journal of Political Theory* (November 2020); https://doi.org/10.1177/1474885120963966.

[41] On this distinction, see Wu Kyŏng-sŏp (우경섭), *Chosŏn chunghwajuŭiŭi sŏnginpgwa tongasia* (조선중화주의의 성립과 동아시아) [*The Formation of Chosŏn Cultural-Centrism and East Asia*] (Seoul: Unistori, 2013), p. 33.

[42] JaHyun K. Haboush, "Constructing the Center: The Ritual Controversy and the Search for a New Identity in Seventeenth-Century Korea," in *Culture and the State in Late Chosŏn Korea*, eds. Haboush and Deuchler, p. 67.

the center of Confucian civilization. What the Korean Neo-Confucians aspired to in the post-Ming context was to turn Chosŏn into "Eastern Zhou" (k. *tongju* 東周).[43] The following statement by Song Siyŏl powerfully represents the late seventeenth-century reformulation of the identity of the Chosŏn state and Korean Neo-Confucians as the carriers of the Confucian Way:

> The [Chinese] people of the Central Plain call us "the Eastern Barbarians" (k. *tongi* 東夷) because we are located in their east. Though the name does not sound beautiful, [whether we become a civilized people] will be determined by whether or not we promote [the Confucian culture of the ancient sages]. Mencius said, "[sage-king] Shun was a man of the East Barbarians and King Wen [who founded the Zhou dynasty] was a man of the Western Barbarians. And yet they all became sages and worthies." [This implies that] we, the country of the East, do not have to worry about not becoming like Zou [Mencius's home country] and Lu [Confucius's home country]. . . . [Seen in this way,] it is solely up to [moral] transformation whether the land of the barbarians of the past can become the land of the civilized people (*xia* 夏) today.[44]

The world-shattering event of the Ming–Qing transition, however, which signaled not merely political change, but, more profoundly, the fundamental relocation of the cultural symbolism that had long defined Korea's moral and cultural identity, did not end with Korean Neo-Confucians' renewed commitment to the Confucian Way per se. It gave rise to a series of philosophical debates, all revolving around how to interpret Confucian classics and Zhu Xi's authoritative commentaries on them. The topics ranged from the cultural–political identity of the Chosŏn state and its statehood under new interstate circumstances, which unfolded in terms of ritual controversy (k. *yesong* 禮訟) on the moral–political standing of the Chosŏn monarch, to more metaphysical questions regarding human nature and, by implication, moral self-cultivation. Such metaphysical questions included: (1) What is the nature of the state of the heart–mind before it becomes engaged with emotion and thought?; (2) Do sages and commoners share the same heart–mind?; and (3) Are the natures of human beings and nonhuman animals identical?[45] While the ritual controversies

---

[43] As noted earlier, the Zhou dynasty was one of the dynasties of the Chinese antiquity, whose humanistic culture Confucius wished to revivify. Song Siyŏl and his Neo-Confucian followers in Korea wanted to transform Chosŏn into an authentic Confucian state (i.e., Zhou) created in the eastern corner of the world. Therefore, in the present context, "Eastern Zhou" does not refer to the second half of the historical Zhou dynasty, commonly known as the Spring and Autumn Period (770–256 BC).

[44] *Songja taejŏn* (宋子大全 131) ("Chamnok"); reprinted from Wu, *Chosŏn chunghwajuŭi*, p. 59 (translation is mine).

[45] See Richard Kim, "Human Nature and Animal Nature: The Horak Debate and Its Philosophical Significance," in *Traditional Korean Philosophy: Problems and Debates*, eds. Youngsun Back and Philip J. Ivanhoe (London: Rowman & Littlefield International, 2017), p. 90.

involved Neo-Confucian scholars from both the mainstream Yulgok school and the T'oegye school,[46] the debates on metaphysical questions mainly engaged the students of Song Siyŏl, many of whom, as noted, influenced Yunjidang's family members and Yunjidang herself in developing their philosophical ideas and political orientations. The Horak debate refers to a series of philosophical debates among the scholars of the Yulgok school on these three metaphysical questions. As will be shown in Section 2, Yunjidang's guiding philosophical concern revolved around the second and third questions.

1.3 The Horak Debate

It goes beyond the scope of this Element to thoroughly examine the Horak debate that continued into the early twentieth century.[47] Since, in the present context, the Horak debate is significant as an intellectual backdrop against which to illuminate the distinctive characteristics of Yunjidang's philosophical thought and intellectual development, let me lay out three important points about the third question of the Horak debate, whether the natures of human beings and nonhuman animals are identical.

First, although it took a purely abstract philosophical form, the Horak debate unfolded during a time when Korean Neo-Confucian intellectuals were grappling with how to address what can be called *the Qing question*, at the heart of which lies the question of how to understand the moral standing of the "barbarians," who Zhu Xi believed were a "species between humans and beasts [whose nature is] hard to change,"[48] and whether they possessed the same nature as humans (belonging to the Confucian civilization). According to Zhu Xi, the natures of human beings and nonhuman animals are fundamentally different. He made this clear when he stated,

> [Nature] that acquires turbid and unbalanced *qi* will become obscured. This is what happens to beasts. *Qi* [can be either] clear [or] turbid. Humans acquire clear *qi* [whereas] beasts acquire turbid *qi*. Humans, for the most part, are fundamentally clear and thus different from beasts. But there are also those who are turbid and so not very different from beasts. … It's simply that he who receives clear *qi* is a sage or worthy – he is like a precious pearl lying in

---

[46] On ritual controversies in seventeenth-century Korea, see Chaihark Hahm, "Ritual and Constitutionalism: Disputing the Ruler's Legitimacy in a Confucian Polity," *American Journal of Comparative Law* 57 (2009), pp. 135–204; Haboush, "Constructing the Center."

[47] For a comprehensive philosophical and historical study on the Horak debate, see Mun Sŏk-yun (문석윤), *Horak nonjaeng hyŏngsŏnggwa chŏn'gae* (호락논쟁 형성과 전개) [*The Origin and Unfolding of the Horak Debate*] (Seoul: Tonggwa sŏ, 2006).

[48] See Hoyt C. Tillman, *Utilitarian Confucianism: Ch'en Liang's Challenge to Chu Hsi* (Cambridge, MA: Council on East Asian Studies, Harvard University, 1982), p. 263, n.7.

crystal clear water. And he who receives turbid *qi* is an idiot or degenerate – he is like a pearl lying in turbid water.[49]

This statement provides one of the foundational premises of Neo-Confucian metaphysics and ethics, to which we shall return repeatedly when discussing the Horak debate and investigating Yunjidang's philosophical thought. What is important in the present context is the fact that Korean Neo-Confucians approached the Qing question, otherwise a political problem, as a quintessential philosophical question in reference to Neo-Confucian metaphysics. More specifically, the problem they were wrestling with revolved around whether the lord–subject relationship established after Chosŏn's humiliating military defeat to Qing in 1636 could be *morally* justified by the moral principle of righteousness, which regulates only *human* relationships. For those who persisted with Song Siyŏl's orthodoxy that the natures of human and nonhuman beings (including "barbarians") are fundamentally different, the moral legitimacy of Qing as the Son of Heaven and the lord–subject relationship between Qing and Chosŏn could never be accepted from a moral standpoint. Since these scholars tended to reside in the Hosŏ region (roughly, the Ch'ungch'ŏng province), they were called the Ho group and distinguished from scholars of the Rak (or Nak) group, based in the Nakha area near Seoul, who supported the thesis that there is no qualitative difference between human beings and nonhuman animals in terms of their original nature. Not surprisingly, some of the scholars from the Nak group not only acknowledged the Jurchens as human beings, equally capable of moral development like Koreans, but actively embraced new philosophical trends and advanced technologies developed in Qing.[50]

Second, the Horak debate also held deep implications for the way in which orthodox Korean Neo-Confucians responded to the social and political crisis resulting from the two devastating wars with the Jurchens. Both wars fundamentally destabilized Korean society's feudal hierarchical order which distinguished the *yangban* class from the commoners (peasants, merchants, and craftsmen) as well as from slaves. In the face of near disintegration of the Chosŏn society, Ho scholars were strongly convinced that the best way to overcome the seventeenth-century political crisis would be to reinforce the ritual-based and heavily gendered hierarchical social order that the ruling elites of Korea had painstakingly restored after the Jurchen invasions; they justified their conservative reform plan

---

[49] Daniel K. Gardner, *Chu Hsi: Learning to Be a Sage* (Berkeley: University of California Press, 1990), p. 98.

[50] See Cho Sŏng-san (조성산), "18segi horak nonjaenggwa noron sasanggyeŭi punhwa 18 (세기 호락논쟁과 노론 사상계의 분화) [The Horak Debate during the Eighteenth Century and the Differentiation within the Dominant Faction of the Yulgok School]," *Han'guk sasangsa hak* 8 (1997), pp. 75–111 (pp.105–108).

in reference to Neo-Confucian metaphysics and the theory of moral self-cultivation. Following Zhu Xi, Ho scholars believed that human nature is originally good in the sense that it is the embodiment of *li*, the universal moral principle.[51] But they also believed that humans are not equal because only those endowed with "clean and pure" *qi*, or who have successfully cultivated themselves through the rigorous practice of Confucian rituals and turned their originally "turbid and impure" *qi* into one that is clear and pure, could become gentlemen. According to them, only gentlemen can possess the moral right to "edify" (and govern) others, namely, uncultivated petty men (*xiaoren* 小人) whose otherwise good nature is obstructed by turbid and impure *qi*.

Ho scholars justified social hierarchy based on moral inequality between gentlemen and petty men while requiring the *yangban* ruling class, understood as a society of gentlemen (and gentlewomen only in their capacity as coparticipants in the patriarchal aristocratic order), to conduct themselves according to the most stringent set of Confucian rituals that were deemed to represent the Heavenly Principle (*tianli* 天理) itself. For them, it was the same moral principle that undergirded the hierarchical relationships between father and son, between ruler and subject, between the Son of Heaven in China and the Chosŏn monarch, and between gentlemen and petty men. This universal yet hierarchical order should never be violated because it was believed to represent "the constant norm" (*jing* 經) of the moral universe.

Nak scholars parted company with the students of Song Siyŏl based in the Hosŏ area, such as Kwŏn Sangha, Song's most prominent student, and Han Wŏnjin (韓元震, 1682–1751), Kwŏn's student whose initial debate with Yi Kan (李柬, 1677–1727), another student of Kwŏn, propelled many rounds of scholarly exchanges that developed into the Horak debate. Song's followers in the Seoul region who sided with Yi Kan, such as Kim Ch'ang-hyŏp (金昌協, 1651–1708), Yi Chae, and Kim Wŏn-haeng (金元行, 1702–72), among others, found the Ho argument deeply problematic and a serious distortion of the Mencian vision of moral development. From a philosophical perspective, the main problem that Nak scholars had with Ho scholars was the latter's interpretation of *qi* primarily as the source of evil that inclines humans to deviate from morality by constituting "the physical nature" (*qizhi zhi xing*, 氣質之性), which obstructs the manifestation of "the original nature" (*benran zhi xing*, 本然之性) that is in essence the *li* itself.[52]

---

[51] On Zhu Xi's cosmological and metaphysical reinterpretation of human nature, see Junghwan Lee, "Zhu Xi's Metaphysical Theory of Human Nature," in *Dao Companion to Zhu Xi's Philosophy*, eds. Kai-chiu Ng and Yong Huang (Dordrecht: Springer, 2020), pp. 265–287.

[52] For a helpful explanation on the original nature and the physical nature in the context of the Horak debate, see Hong Jung Geun, "Is the Morality of Human Beings Superior to the Morality

Nak scholars did not necessarily object to this metaphysical distinction between the original nature, which is Heaven-decreed and thus as purely good as *li* itself, and the physical nature that contains the source of evil. What they objected to was Ho scholars' pronounced attention to the physical nature or the inextricable intertwinement between the physical nature and the original nature, with the effect of fundamentally distinguishing humans, born with clear and pure *qi*, from nonhuman animals and the myriad "things" (*wu* 物) in the universe that are born/created with *qi* of lower qualities.[53] Practically speaking, the strong emphasis on *qi* as the marker between human beings and nonhuman animals led to the parallel accentuation of radical differences among humans – between those who are born with a clear and pure physical nature, on the one hand, and those who are not, on the other – with a strong implication that those who are born with turbid and imbalanced *qi*, namely, the petty men, have innate obstacles that keep them from becoming gentlemen. As Nak scholars saw it, however, the moral and normative significance of the original nature, which is shared by all beings and things in the universe as *li*, could never be obscured or diminished by the empirical force of the physical nature, and insomuch as *all* humans (and nonhuman beings) are born with the original nature that is purely good, all should be thought capable of the five cardinal moral virtues that inhere in the (original) nature.[54] For them, Ho scholars' interpretation of Zhu Xi's account of human nature would critically undermine Confucian moral universalism, at the core of which lies moral transformability of *all*, regardless of one's endowment of *qi* or social background.

Moreover, and third, at least for some Nak scholars, the Ho argument that lent strong support for rigid hierarchical order did not sit comfortably with the growing "egalitarian" trend of late Chosŏn Korea in which merchants and craftsmen, social groups that had long been discriminated against despite their legal status as "commoners," emerged along with affluent peasantries equipped with novel agricultural methods and advanced technologies as a new social force that galvanized the Korean economy, precipitating the urbanization of Seoul, the capital city of Chosŏn. Although it is certainly far-fetched to say that

---

of Non-Human Beings? Debate over Human versus Animal Nature in the Joseon Period," *Korea Journal* 51:1 (2011), pp. 72–96 (pp. 76–78).

[53] It is worth noting that the initial debate between Han Wŏnjin and Yi Kan began with the question of whether the inactivated state of the mind contains only the original nature or the physical nature as well. While Han took the view that *qi* is also constitutive of the inactivated mind or the mind's substance, Yi contended that the original nature alone constitutes the inactivated mind and therefore the inactivated mind is purely good. See Lee Cheon Sung, "Philosophical Implications of the Discussion of *Mibal* in the Horak Debate of the Late Joseon Period," *Korea Journal* 51:1 (2011), pp. 97–117; Kim, "Human Nature and Animal Nature," pp. 90–92.

[54] The five cardinal virtues (*wu chang*, 五常) include benevolence (*ren*), righteousness (*yi*), ritual propriety (*li**), wisdom (*zhi*), and trustworthiness (*xin* 信).

Nak scholars actively pursued social egalitarianism,[55] some of a more progressive group of scholars from an eighteenth-century Nak faction, widely known as the Pukhakp'a (北學派, the Northern Learning School), did indeed explore the drastic restructuring of Chosŏn's feudal order into a more meritocratic and egalitarian society in which everyone qua human being could engage in moral self-development. Some more radical members of this group went further and advocated freeing slaves that belonged to the government and abolishing discrimination against illegitimate sons (i.e., those who were born of a *yangban* father and his non*yangban* concubine) who were blocked from entering the government, which had long been a major social problem in Chosŏn society. If we understand the kernel of the moral project pushed by the Northern Learning scholars in terms of "the universal expansion of goodness,"[56] it is hardly coincidental that some prominent members of this school such as Hong Tae-yong (洪大容, 1731–83) and Pak Chi-wŏn (朴趾源, 1737–1805) tried to overcome the orthodox Neo-Confucian account of *hua–yi*, which stipulated that the *qi* of the "barbarians" was such that they could not become morally cultivated and thus civilized.

1.4 From Im Sŏngju to Im Yunjidang

Finally, before delving into Yunjidang's philosophical thought, a brief discussion about Im Sŏngju seems necessary, not only because of his distinctive philosophical stance in the midst of the Horak debate but also because of his strong influence on his sister's scholarship.[57]

As noted, Im Sŏngju studied under the guidance of Yi Chae, one of the core members of the Nak school. Some contemporary scholars, therefore, associate Im's philosophical position with the Nak argument. Indeed, like many of the

---

[55] Their eminent concern still consisted in the philosophical inquiry of human nature and its implications for the moral self-cultivation of members of the *yangban* class (Cho, "18segi horaknonjaeng," p. 85). Some Nak scholars, therefore, were deeply worried that the Nak argument could evolve into a radical proposal to reconstitute Chosŏn's ritual-based, hierarchical Neo-Confucian society. See Lee Kyungku, "The Horak Debate from the Reign of King Sukjong to King Sunjo," *Korea Journal* 51:1 (2011), pp. 15–41 (pp. 33–34).

[56] Yi Wan-chae (이완재), "Songnihagŭi maengnak'esŏ pon ch'ogi kaehwa sasang (성리학의 맥락에서 본 초기개화사상) [The Early Enlightenment Thought from the Standpoint of Cheng-Zhu Neo-Confucian Philosophy]," *Tongasia muhwa yŏn'gu* 29 (1996), pp. 127–157 (p. 144).

[57] For studies on Im Sŏngju's philosophical influence on Yunjidang, see Kim Chae-im (김재임), "Im yunjidangŭi songnironŭl t'onghae pon in'ganhak kujo (임윤지당의 성리론을 통해 본 인간학 구조) [Im Yunjidang's Neo-Confucian Philosophy of Human Nature and the Structure of Her Philosophical Understanding of Human Being]," *Kangwŏn munhwa yŏn'gu* 26 (2007), pp. 173–188; Kim Mi-yŏng (김미영), "Sŏngnihak'esŏ taedudoen kongchŏk yŏngyŏge taehan yŏsŏngjuŭijŏk chŏpkkŭn (성리학에서 대두된 '공적영역'에 대한 여성주의적 접근) [A Feminist Approach to the Question of 'Public Sphere' in the Cheng-Zhu Neo-Confucian Context]," *Ch'ŏrak yŏn'gu* 29 (2005), pp. 389–416.

Nak scholars, Im Sŏngju was against the rigid social hierarchy espoused by the Ho scholars. For instance, when he was appointed as a local magistrate, he issued the following statement to office clerks, members of the "middle men" (k. *chung'in* 中人), the class between the *yangban* and commoners:

> In giving birth to human beings, Heaven equally bestowed them the moral principles of benevolence and righteousness. Though you are mere office clerks, how could there be any difference only in your case? Recently, in dealing with office clerks, local magistrates did not rely on the method of moral edification but [rather] punished them cruelly unless those office clerks employed immoral means [to please them]. This situation is something of which you should be deeply ashamed. As far as I am concerned, I will treat you with sincerity and trustworthiness and encourage both you and myself mutually with the feeling of shame.[58] As for you, you must make every effort to get rid of old wrongs and to expand your new understandings. You must treat yourselves as if you were gentlemen (k. *sagunja* 士君子).[59]

> [天之生人, 均賦仁義. 雖爾胥吏, 何獨異乎. 近來爲守宰者,待胥吏以化外, 不以權數愚之則必用刑杖虐之. 此實爾輩羞恥事也. 余則欲以誠信相待, 廉恥相勉. 爾輩各宜自礪滌其舊染, 而發其新知, 自持其身, 如士君子.]

Although it appears that Im Sŏngju maintained his egalitarian stance toward moral self-development into his later days, he established his own philosophical position, which he distinguished not only from the Ho argument but also from the Nak argument. What is central to Im Sŏngju's argument is the rejection of the metaphysical distinction between the original nature and the physical nature, the shared Neo-Confucian assumption held by both Ho and Nak scholars. According to Im Sŏngju, there is only one human nature and it is wherein *li* dwells with a specific physical endowment, making the distinction between the original nature and the physical nature pointless. Otherwise stated, for Im Sŏngju human nature cannot be conceived of separated from *qi*.[60] Remarkably, then, he contends that the physical nature is itself the original nature, further implying that there is no qualitative distinction between *li* and *qi*, as *li* can never be separated from *qi* and vice versa.[61] In Im Sŏngju's view, therefore, *qi* cannot be understood as the source of evil as the Ho scholars believed, because, in its purest state, *qi* is also good, as clearly evidenced by Mencius's famous notion of "flood-like *qi*" (*haoran zhi qi* 浩然之氣).[62]

---

[58] According to Mencius, the feeling of shame is the sprout of righteousness (*Mencius* 2A6).

[59] Im Sŏngju (임성주), *Nongmunjip* (鹿門集) [*The Collected Writings of Im Sŏngju*], 1014a. For the original Chinese text of the *Nongmunjip*, I consulted the digital text remastered at the Korean Classics database, https://db.itkc.or.kr/dir/item?itemId=MO#/dir/node?dataId=ITKC_MO_0532A; the translation is mine.

[60] *Nongmunjip* 408c.   [61] *Nongmunjip* 270c.   [62] *Mencius* 2A2.

In the end, the idea that *li* and *qi* are equal in substance and that the physical nature is itself the original nature led Im Sŏngju to advance his distinctive metaphysical theory, which goes beyond the Horak debate. Consider the following statement by Im:

> In my view, that water flows downward; it is water's original nature. It is also the Great Ultimate that water is endowed with. That fire is burning upward; it is fire's original nature. It is also the Great Ultimate that fire is endowed with. This points to the so-called Heaven-decreed nature and this is so-called the nature that dogs, cows, and humans have. If we speak about this [nature or *li*] comprehensively, there is [only] one nature that underlies all under Heaven and this shows that *li* is one (i.e., the whole substance of the Great Ultimate). [However,] if we speak about it from the standpoint of its differentiation, each of myriad things has its own nature and this shows the difference that the differentiation [of *li* involves] (i.e., the Great Ultimate each being or thing is endowed with). To speak of it comprehensively, myriad things are endowed with one [principle]; to speak of it from the standpoint of its differentiation, one is included within [each of] myriad things. In fact, therefore, [*li* as one and the *li* that myriad things are endowed with] do not refer to two different things. It only means that nature refers to what a being/thing each has originally received [from Heaven]. It was said that "each has received the right Heaven-decreed nature" and "each possesses its distinctive nature," and this means that it is indeed the case that all beings and things are different from each other. . . . How could there be two different kinds of nature like the original nature and the physical nature?[63]

> [區區之意則只以爲水之潤下, 卽水之本性. 而亦水之所具之太極也. 火之炎上, 卽火之本性. 而亦火之所具之太極也. 此卽所謂天命之性, 此卽所謂犬牛人之性. 蓋合而言之則通天下一性, 卽理之一也 (統體太極). 分而言之則萬物各一其性, 乃分之殊也 (各具太極). 雖曰合焉而一之中萬者具焉, 雖曰分焉而萬之中一者包焉, 實非有二物也. 只是性者, 本以物之所受而名之者. 旣曰各正性命, 各一其性. 則物之不齊, 固物之情也. . . . 烏在其本然氣質之非二性也哉.]

Here, Im Sŏngju presents several important points, which, as will be shown in Section 2, strongly influenced Yunjidang's philosophical thought. First, the Heaven-decreed nature (*tianming zhi xing* 天命之性) that Zhu Xi famously understood in terms of *li* or the original nature is in fact the nature that defines the nature of each being or thing that is embodied with *qi*. And this Heaven-decreed nature is what constitutes each species' nature. Second, *li*, which is nothing other than the Great Ultimate (*taiji* 太極), the metaphysical pivot of the cosmos, has two dimensions: While, on the one hand, it is *one* universal moral principle that constitutes the nature of all things and beings in the moral universe, it is simultaneously manifested differently in the particularized nature of each thing

---

or being because of its distinctive endowment of *qi*. Third, there is no qualitative difference between *li* as the universal moral principle and *li* as embodied in each concrete being and thing. And yet, *li*, which is embodied in the specific being or thing of a distinctive quality of *qi*, cannot be the nature that constitutes the original nature (or the Heaven-decreed nature) that exists in separation from the physical nature, as the participants of the Horak debate believe. *Li*'s cosmic oneness notwithstanding, insomuch as it forms the nature of each being or thing, it cannot but be the physical nature that differentiates one from the others. To the extent that each being or thing is each endowed with the Heaven-given nature that is distinctive in its core characteristics, it cannot be claimed that the natures of human beings and nonhuman animals (and other myriad things) are identical. All beings and things are different precisely in this sense.[64]

Thus understood, Im Sŏngju distanced himself from both Ho and Nak scholars as far as his mature philosophy was concerned, by developing his own distinctive argument for the difference between the natures of human beings and nonhuman animals. That is, while maintaining the egalitarian moral stance that he learned from the Nak argument in regard to the possibility of moral self-development, Im arrived at a philosophical position that is similar to the Ho argument as far as the third question of the Horak debate was concerned – yet from completely different philosophical grounds that were still nested within the Neo-Confucian philosophical framework provided by Zhu Xi. Ultimately, Im Sŏngju's philosophical originality boils down to his idea of *qi* as originally good, which undergirds his monistic Neo-Confucian philosophy that highlights the inseparability between *li* and *qi*, making the latter tantamount to the Great Ultimate itself.[65] It is this monistic metaphysical system of Neo-Confucianism that inspired Yunjidang to develop her own philosophical reflections on Confucian classics and, by extension, the Horak debate, and ultimately to wrestle with the possibility of female sagehood.

2 Im Yunjidang's Neo-Confucian Philosophy

2.1 Metaphysical Monism

Neo-Confucianism refers to a new mode of Confucianism that emerged during the Song dynasty, introduced by scholars who reformulated classical

---

[64] For a thorough reconstruction and exposition of Im Sŏngju's philosophical thought, see Son Hŭng-ch'ŏl (손흥철), *Nongmun im sŏngjuŭi sam'gwa ch'ŏrak* (녹문 임성주의 삶과 철학) [*The Life and Philosophy of Im Sŏngju*] (Seoul: Chisik sanŏpsa, 2004).

[65] It was Zhu Xi who first interpreted the Great Ultimate as *li* in the course of grappling with Zhou Dunyi's "Discussion of the Taiji Diagram" (*Taijitu shuo* 太極圖說). See Joseph A. Adler, *Reconstructing the Confucian Dao: Zhu Xi's Appropriation of Zhou Dunyi* (Albany: State University of New York Press, 2014).

Confucianism – Mencian Confucianism in particular, mainly focused on ethics and political philosophy – into a cosmological and mesmerizingly metaphysical philosophy in which cosmology and ethics, metaphysics and ethics, and ethics and political theory were inextricably entwined, creating a seamlessly interconnected system of oneness. Although it is certainly not true that Song Neo-Confucians subscribed to the same philosophical ideas and political visions, the key characteristics of Neo-Confucianism as described above are found most saliently in Cheng-Zhu Neo-Confucianism, which became the dominant intellectual trend and political ideology during the Ming dynasty. It is this version of Neo-Confucianism, synthesized by Zhu Xi, that inspired the founding of Chosŏn and its subsequent Confucian transformation.

As followers of Mencius, Neo-Confucians all agreed with his idea that human nature is good. But the intellectual struggle with and unintended influences from Daoism, and especially Buddhism, led them to redefine the goodness of human nature in cosmological–metaphysical terms, by which Mencius had originally meant the presence of moral sentiments within human nature that incline one toward goodness. That is, Neo-Confucians held that humans are originally good in the sense that they are born with a Heaven-bestowed moral nature, which is none other than the universal moral principle. What is interesting is that Neo-Confucians believed that the moral principle that constitutes human nature also defines the nature of all other beings and things in the universe – together they were called *wu* – and that it is this very principle, sometimes called the Heavenly Principle, that simultaneously predicates the entire cosmos. For Neo-Confucians, therefore, the principle was at once normative–moral and descriptive–ontological, seamlessly interweaving the metaphysical and empirical worlds as well as cosmological and moral principles. Following Zhu Xi, Neo-Confucians understood the Great Ultimate, the pivot of the cosmos, as principle and they likewise defined the original human nature in terms of principle. For this reason, Cheng-Zhu Neo-Confucianism was also called the Learning of Principle (*lixue* 理學).

This does not mean that Neo-Confucians dismissed the importance of *qi*. In fact, Zhou Dunyi 周敦頤, (1017–73), one of the progenitors of Song Neo-Confucianism, explained the origin of the universe and the myriad things in it in terms of the movement and stillness of the Great Ultimate, which generates *yin* and *yang*, the two main modalities of *qi* as the vital force that makes up the natural world. In general, Neo-Confucians embraced the Han theory of *yin–yang*, which explained the spawning of the so-called Five Phases (*wuxing* 五行) and the subsequent creation of the myriad things, including human beings, in terms of active and ceaseless interactions between *yin* and *yang*. Yet, Song Neo-Confucians distinguished themselves from Han Confucians, as well as their contemporary Daoist and Buddhist rivals, by presenting principle as the moral–normative pattern or standard that underlies the world made of *qi*. Moreover, extending the *li–qi* metaphysics to the philosophical understanding of human nature, Neo-Confucians distinguished the original nature, the embodiment of the Heavenly Principle in the heart–mind that is purely good, from the physical nature that contains the physical endowment of *qi*. They explained the Confucian ethical project of moral self-cultivation as the slow and painstaking process in which one recovers his/her original nature by overcoming his/her physical nature, which is murky, impure, or imbalanced, blocking the original good nature within. As discussed in the previous section, the orthodox Neo-Confucians of eighteenth-century Korea, all devout followers of Zhu Xi, wrestled with the three questions that guided the unfolding of the Horak debate under these core Neo-Confucian assumptions. Regardless of their scholarly affiliation with the Ho or Nak argument, Korean Neo-Confucians generally held the dualistic understanding of *li* and *qi* as well as of the original nature and the physical nature. In a nutshell, the dividing line between the Ho and Nak groups was their differing understandings of the Heaven-decreed nature – whether it contains the physical nature and thus whether it should be understood as purely good.

Yunjidang was markedly differentiated from the mainstream Korean Neo-Confucians of her time in that she rejected the dualistic understanding of *li* and *qi*.

> *Li* is *qi*'s substance and *qi* is what contains *li*. This means that they are one while being two and they are two while being one. Many people misunderstand Zhu Xi's statement that "*li* exists prior to *qi*" and believe that the Great Ultimate is something like a circle that transcends physical endowments. This is deeply wrong. Without *qi*, what else can be there for principle to ride on and achieve its harmonious operation? The Great Ultimate is nothing more than the principle of *yin* and *yang* and it is not that there exists a principle independently of *yin* and *yang*. *Li* (as principle) is just the spontaneous operation of *yin* and *yang*. The Great Ultimate refers to the state where *li* has reached at its utmost point to which nothing can be further added. Without *li*, there is indeed no place from which *qi* can spring and, yet, without *qi*, where can *li*, too, spring from and exist? Therefore, one can understand this [complex relationship between *li* and *qi*] from the perspective of *qi*. [*Li* and *qi*] can be neither separated nor combined and they can be neither divided nor welded.[66]

> [夫理者, 氣之體也. 氣者, 理之器也. 此一而二, 二而一者也. 人多誤認朱子有是理而後有是氣之訓, 乃以太極爲超形氣一圓圈之物. 甚不然也. 無其氣, 則理何從掛搭而成造化乎. 太極不過陰陽之理, 非陰陽之外, 別有

---

[66] *Yunjidang yugo* 26a–b.

簡理耳. 只是陰陽之自然如此之謂理也. 其理之至極無加之謂太極也. 非
理氣固無所自, 而非氣理又何從而有乎. 只卽氣而認取其意思而已可也.
無離合, 無分段, 無罅縫.]

In Yunjidang's view, Zhu Xi's statement that "*li* exists prior to *qi*" must not be understood literally, as if *li* and *qi* were two separate things with the former having both temporal and normative priority over the latter. This common misunderstanding stems from the failure to understand that the Great Ultimate is the principle that is cosmic and universal, and that this cosmic and universal moral principle is nothing more than the principle revealed in the spontaneous operations of *yin* and *yang* that are *qi*. What this implies is that as principle, *li* is not so much a transcendental form or idea, to use Platonic language, that exists outside the physical world and the myriad things in it, but something that is inextricably intertwined with *qi* which composes the physical world. However, Yunjidang does not relegate principle to a mere attribute of *yin* and *yang* or to the pattern internal to their dynamic interactions which, as Zhou Dunyi explained, gives birth to the myriad things. The point Yunjidang is trying to make here is that there is no qualitative difference between *li* and *qi*. That is, from the standpoint of *qi*, *li* is always the principle of *qi*, not something that wholly transcends it.[67]

Nevertheless, when she explains the difference between human beings and nonhuman animals and other things in the universe, Yunjidang still relies on the traditional Neo-Confucian analytical framework of *li* and *qi*, understanding the latter as the source of moral difference. Like other Neo-Confucians, Yunjidang believes that every being and thing in the universe is born with the principle that constitutes the nature in which the five cardinal human virtues reside: namely, benevolence, righteousness, ritual propriety, wisdom, and trustworthiness. Although the differences of *qi* give rise to moral differences between humans who are born with "balanced (*zheng* 正) and clear (*tong* 通)" *qi* and nonhuman animals and nonliving things that are endowed with "imbalanced (*pian* 偏) and murky (*sai* 塞)" *qi* in terms of capability of developing innate moralities, such differences do not obliterate the fact that nonhuman animals and nonliving things share the same nature bestowed by Heaven.[68]

Yunjidang, however, departs from the mainstream Yulgok school that upholds the thesis that "the substance of [principle that constitutes the nature of a being/thing] is complete but its functions are limited" (k. *ch'ejŏn yong*

---

[67] Therefore, I disagree with Lee Hae-Im, when he states, "I believe that Im Yunjidang set the relationship between principle and the material in terms of cause and effect." See Hae-Im Lee, "Im Yunjidang's View of Material Composition," *Journal of Confucian Philosophy and Culture* 34 (2020), pp. 105–128 (p. 109).

[68] *Yunjidang yugo* 28b–29a.

pudal 體全用不達) from her distinctive perspective of metaphysical monism. According to the Yulgok school, principle is completely good, and thus it cannot contain anything that makes humans (or other beings and things) deviate from morality. Yet, because of the impurity or turbidity of *qi* (or the physical nature) that one is born with, his/her original nature (as principle) is blocked from manifesting itself in its original form. In Yunjidang's view, this established view fails to note that in its purest form, *qi*, like principle, is good in itself, the central premise of Im Sŏngju's entire philosophical system, as we saw in Section 1.[69] This also implies that mainstream Korean Neo-Confucians are at fault in dividing human nature into the original nature and the physical nature and attributing the goodness (or "being complete") only to the original nature, resulting in the problematic conclusion that the physical nature is an obstacle preventing full moral realization of the original nature.

Apparently under the strong influence of her brother, Yunjidang submits a radical reinterpretation of the Heaven-decreed nature, which the mainstream Korean Neo-Confucians of the Yulgok school had long associated with the original nature.

> It is because of the original [nature] decreed by Heaven that all things and beings are different. They each form [their] own distinctive nature in accordance with [their] physical endowments and this explains the statement that "each being/thing is equipped with the Great Ultimate." And this refers to the very nature [that we find in the canonical Neo-Confucian statement that] "nature is principle." How can there be another nature independent of this nature, allowing one to say [wrongly] that originally there is no [Heaven-]decreed nature or to suspect that principle is limited by *qi*? In general, those living things that do not possess the *qi* of blood and lack cognitive ability such as grass and tree each have received physical endowments that are the most imbalanced and turbid. Therefore, as for the principle residing in each being/thing, it becomes that particular being's/thing's distinctive principle in accordance with its distinctive physical endowments.[70]

> [物之不齊,乃天命之本然也.隨其氣質而自爲一性, 則此是各具太極也. 卽此是性, 卽理之性也. 豈可外此討性, 而或謂之原無命性, 或疑其理爲 氣局耶. 蓋凡生物之無血氣而無所知覺, 如草木之類者, 又得其形氣之偏 塞之偏塞者. 故理之在是物者, 亦隨其形氣而自爲一物之理.]

Central to Yunjidang's argument is that the original nature, as decreed by Heaven, cannot be conceived of in separation from the physical endowments of *qi* that each being or thing is born with. According to Yunjidang, there is no original nature to be limited by the physical nature that keeps one from becoming good. The Heaven-decreed nature is itself entwined with distinctive

---

[69] *Yunjidang yugo* 32a–b. [70] *Yunjidang yugo* 29a.

physical endowments and the principle that constitutes human nature is always a distinctive one shaped by *qi*, not limited by it. In short, there is only one Heaven-decreed and original human nature and it is nothing other than the physical nature that contains its distinctive principle. Yunjidang's criticism of the thesis that "the substance of principle is complete but its functions are limited" is most pronounced in the following statement:

> As for how Heaven creates things, they always have a norm. Once the various physical endowments are assigned, then the norms governing things are no longer the same. This is how things ought to be according to principle. How can it be said that the substance [of principle] is complete but its functions are limited? If one talks from the perspective of principle about the beginning of life, then human beings and other things all have a single source. Hence the saying that the unified body of the myriad things is one Great Ultimate. Yet, if one looks at [nature] from the perspective of *qi* after things have come into being, each has its own particular nature. Hence the saying that myriad things each possess one Great Ultimate. The statement that "everything obtains its correct nature as decreed [by Heaven]" refers to this.[71]
>
> [夫天之生物, 必有其則.形氣既殊, 則則各不同. 亦理所當然者也. 又何可謂體全而用不達乎. 以理而語其生之始, 則人與物同一源. 故曰萬物統體一太極. 以氣而觀其生之後, 則物物各一其性. 故曰萬物各具一太極. 此之謂各正性命也.]

From Yunjidang's standpoint, Nak scholars are misguided because their preoccupation with the universal force of principle and the good original nature keeps them from seeing the undeniable difference between human and nonhuman animals in terms of the Heaven-decreed nature. At the same time, she criticizes Ho scholars for misunderstanding *qi* as the force limiting or distorting the natural operation of the original nature toward goodness. What both groups of scholars failed to realize is the fact that there exists only a concrete and embodied nature that is specific to a particular species or category of things. There is neither an abstract, transcendent nature separate from one's physical embodiment nor a physical nature that is devoid of Heaven's decree, the Great Ultimate, or the principle. For Yunjidang, the physical nature is itself the original nature precisely in this sense.

Yunjidang's criticism of the Yulgok school's *li–qi* theory, then, eventually prompted her to critically revisit the Neo-Confucian notion that "the principle is one and its particularizations are many" (*liyi fenshu* 理一分殊).[72] Among

---

[71] *Yunjidang yugo* 30a.

[72] For a helpful introduction of this notion first stated by Cheng I and further developed by Zhu Xi, see Stephen C. Angle and Justin Tiwald, *Neo-Confucianism: A Philosophical Introduction* (Cambridge: Polity, 2017), pp. 31–33.

eighteenth-century Korean Neo-Confucians, the dominant view was that while there is a single source of goodness represented by one universal principle or, expressed differently, as the Great Ultimate, its manifold manifestations through the natures of the myriad things should mean that the manifestation of principle in each concrete being or thing is imperfect because it is limited by *qi*. Otherwise stated, Korean Neo-Confucians noted an abyssal normative gap between the cosmic universality of principle as the Great Ultimate, on the one side, and its specific manifestations in the concrete and physically embodied beings and things, on the other – the natural corollary of their dualistic under-standing of *li* and *qi*. Yunjidang countered this dominant position, avidly supported by Ho scholars, as follows:

> It would be gravely wrong, if someone says the following: even though benevolence, righteousness, ritual propriety, and wisdom constitute the nature that is shared by both humans and nonhuman animals and things, the reason that nonhuman animals and things are unable to reveal their posses-sion of them is because of the constraints of *qi*, which renders the functions [of principle] incomplete and, therefore, [the natures that they possess are] not their original natures. The reason would be transparent if one only considers the phrase "the principle is one and its particularizations are many." The principle in "the principle is one" indeed refers to *li*. How would the principle in "its manifold particularizations" alone not refer to the (same) *li*? [Therefore,] the expression "its particularizations are many" must be understood as referring to principle. Many people, however, under-stand "manifold particularizations" from the perspective of *qi* and [thus wrongly] associate "one" with principle and "manifold particularizations" with *qi*, going so far as to claim that "the substance [of principle] is complete but its functions are limited." This, too, is incorrect.[73]

> [若曰, 仁義禮智, 卽人物所同之性也, 而物之不見有仁義之性者, 爲氣所局而用不達而已, 非本然之體也云爾, 則大不然. 此於理一分殊四字上著眼, 却自分明. 理一之理, 固理也. 而分殊之理, 獨非理乎.分殊字, 亦當屬理字. 今人多屬氣字看, 以爲一者, 理也, 分者, 氣也.至有體全用不達之語. 誤矣.]

According to Yunjidang, by associating metaphysical oneness with *li* and *li*'s manifold particularizations in the myriad things with *qi*, the existing scholarship fails to understand that there is no qualitative difference between one universal principle and its concrete and manifold particularizations. However, Yunjidang's focus seems to be not so much on the cosmic metaphysical oneness as such but the normative implications of the fact that there is no qualitative difference between *li* as one universal principle and the *li* that has been

---

[73] *Yunjidang yugo* 31a.

particularized in concrete beings and things: that every being and thing in the universe possesses a distinctive nature and their natures, which are different from one another because of different physical endowments, wholly contain the same universal principle. A further implication is that outside this concrete embodiment there is no principle. Again, for Yunjidang, there can be no abstract and transcendent principle that is a priori, unpalpable, or unspecific.

Some Korean scholars understand Yunjidang as a feminist, based on her bold reinterpretation of Neo-Confucian *li–qi* metaphysics, by paying strong attention to the physical nature as particularistic embodiments of an otherwise single universal principle.[74] There is an ongoing debate as to whether or in what sense Yunjidang can be understood as a feminist thinker and we will turn to this question in the next section. It suffices here, though, to say that Yunjidang's metaphysical monism is deeply indebted to Im Sŏngju and therefore, unless one is ready to claim that Im Sŏngju, too, was a feminist thinker, it would be premature to understand Yunjidang as a feminist simply based on the distinctive mode of her metaphysical thinking which was markedly different from the mainstream account of Neo-Confucianism widely held by (male) scholars belonging to the Yulgok school. What is important in the present context is that Yunjidang developed her metaphysical monism in the course of grappling with some of the central questions raised during the Horak debate – particularly, the question of whether human beings and nonhuman animals (and nonliving things) possess the same nature. My discussion thus far reveals that Yunjidang believed that the natures of human beings and nonhuman animals are not identical without associating the Heaven-decreed nature only with the former. I now turn to how she extended her metaphysical monism to the Confucian ethics of moral self-cultivation and the arguments she made in relation to women's moral agency.

2.2 Neo-Confucian Moral Self-Cultivation

Neo-Confucianism holds that principle constitutes the nature and, as noted, it calls this purely good nature the original nature.[75] The problem is that as principle, the original nature has no moral agency, though it contains the

---

[74] See, for instance, Kim Sesŏria (김세서리아), "Chosŏn sŏngnihagŭi t'aegŭk ŭmyangnonŭl t'onghae pon han'gukchŏk yŏsŏng chuch'e hyŏngsŏng iron mosaek (조선 성리학의 태극음 양론을 통해 본 한국적 여성주체형성 이론 모색) [A Search for the Theory of Korean Female Subjectivity Formation through the Discourses of the Great Ultimate and *Yin–Yang*]," *Yuhak yŏn'gu* 36 (2016), pp. 295–315.

[75] A portion of this section has been reproduced, with substantial modifications, from Sungmoon Kim, "The Way to Become a Female Sage: Im Yunjidang's Confucian Feminism," *Journal of the History of Ideas* 75:3 (2014), pp. 395–416. I am grateful to the University of Pennsylvania Press for permission to reprint the relevant part of this essay.

principles of morality.[76] Rather, in Neo-Confucianism moral agency is understood as the property of the heart–mind in which nature dwells, often obfuscated by *qi* or the physical nature that generates all kinds of human desires and emotions. Yunjidang explains the distinction between the nature and the heart–mind as follows:

> Generally speaking, nature is the principle that is contained in the heart–mind and heart–mind is a bowl that contains the nature. They are separated, but also united. . . . Principle has no action, but the heart–mind does. Principle leaves no trace, but the heart–mind does. If not for principle, there is nothing to be shined forth. If not for the heart–mind, there is nothing that can shine forth [the principle within].[77]

> [夫性也者,心之所具之理,心也者,性之所寓之器. 二而一者也. . . . 理無爲 而心有爲. 理無迹而心有迹. 非理, 無所發. 非心, 不能發.]

Corresponding with their dualistic approach to the original nature and the physical nature, Song Neo-Confucians likewise understood the heart–mind in dualistic terms, conceptualizing two different kinds of heart–mind – the heart–mind of the Way (*daoxin* 道心), a moral mind that contains principle and has both the intention and the power to overcome human desires (*renyu* 人慾), and the human heart–mind (*renxin* 人心), which is nothing but human desires stemming from the physical nature. Zhu Xi famously reformulates Confucian moral self-cultivation in terms of overcoming the human heart–mind and thereby preserving the heart–mind of the Way (and the principle therein). Zhu Xi says,

> [I]f we may distinguish between the human heart–mind and the heart–mind of the Way, the former arises from the self-centeredness of the *qi* of the physical body, while the latter originates from the correctness of the nature and mandate, and this is why, in terms of their awareness, they are not the same. . . . [A]mong human beings, none fail to possess a physical form, and therefore, even those of the highest wisdom cannot but possess a human heart–mind; moreover, none fail to possess a nature, and so, even those of the lowest intelligence cannot but possess the heart–mind of the Way. . . . If you are focused and refined, then you will carefully examine the two and not mix

---

[76] According to Zhu Xi, "Nature is correct principle. Benevolence, righteousness, [ritual] propriety, and wisdom are all contained therein" (Chu Hsi, *Learning to Be a Sage*, p. 98). Zhu Xi also says that the heart–mind is a master (*zhuzai* 主宰). See Curie Virág, "Moral Psychology and Cultivating the Self," in *Zhu Xi: Selected Writings*, ed. Philip J. Ivanhoe (New York: Oxford University Press, 2019), p. 9.

[77] *Yunjidang yugo* 39b–40a. The idea of "separate but united" also shows the monistic structure of Yunjidang's philosophical thought. Zhu Xi offers a similar explanation when he says, "The heart–mind as it is in itself is the nature. . . . We can say that the heart–mind is replete with all pattern–principle and that the nature is the reason for this being so" (Philip J. Ivanhoe, "Metaphysics, Epistemology, and Ethics," in Ivanhoe [ed.], *Zhu Xi*, p. 20).

them up. If you are single-minded, then you will protect the correctness of your original heart–mind and not depart from it. If you pursue your affairs from this perspective, and do not desist for even a moment, then inevitably the heart–mind of the Way will become the master of your person, and your human heart–mind will in every instance obey the mandate.[78]

Yunjidang was no different from other Neo-Confucians as far as the distinction between the heart–mind of the Way and the human heart–mind was concerned, as clearly evidenced in the following statement: "The human heart–mind arises from private [desires] grounded in physical endowments while the heart–mind of the Way originates from the correct nature decreed [by Heaven]."[79] Like her Chinese Neo-Confucian predecessors, then, Yunjidang understood the gist of moral self-cultivation in terms of recovering one's heart–mind of the Way by overcoming the human heart–mind, and she was convinced that in overcoming the human heart–mind nothing is more important than practicing ritual propriety as meticulously as possible.

Yunjidang upheld the Neo-Confucian reformulation of ritual propriety as the cultural articulation of the Heavenly Principle, underpinning the constant standard for all human conduct.[80] She believed that the rigorous practice of ritual propriety, with full reverential attention (*jing* 敬) toward the Way (or principle), would enable anyone to become good.[81] Interpreting *Analects* 12.1 where Confucius famously defines the virtue of benevolence with reference to ritual propriety,[82] Yunjidang expressed her faith in the intrinsic connection between ritual propriety and human moral perfectibility as follows:

The sages are the same in kind as I am.[83] Most people are the same as the sages in being endowed with the principles of the Great Ultimate as their nature. It is only because of the constraints imposed by their endowments of *qi* or the obscuration of self-centered desires for material things that there are differences between the wise and the foolish, the worthy and the unworthy. Nevertheless, in terms of their original natures, they are the same. And so, those who have awakened understand that their nature is the same as that of Yao or Shun and that they will succeed in their search to attain it; like travelers seeking their homes, or diners seeking to be full, they will attain their aspiration to become sages. As for describing the sages, the most we can say is that they are "great and fully transformed."[84] Mencius said, "Everyone can become a Yao or a Shun."[85] If everyone can become a Yao or a Shun, how

---

[78] Virág, "Moral Psychology and Cultivating the Self," p. 41.

[79] *Yunjidang yugo* 39a (人心者, 生於形氣之私者也. 道心者, 原於性命之正者也).

[80] *Yunjidang yugo* 40a (夫禮者, 天理之節文, 人事之儀則, 所以立人道者也).

[81] For Yunjidang's emphasis on reverential attention, see *Yunjidang yugo* 41a.

[82] "Restraining the self and returning to ritual propriety (*keji fuli** 克己復禮) constitutes benevolence (*ren*)" (translation is mine).

[83] *Mencius* 6A7.   [84] *Mencius* 7B25.   [85] *Mencius* 6B2.

much more possible is this for Yanzi [Yan Yuan], who had the abilities of a secondary sage! Since this is the case, those who aspire to become a sage should first seek what Yanzi took joy in. Those who seek what Yanzi took joy in should first learn from Yanzi's love of learning. What is it to love learning? It is nothing more than to observe [what Confucius calls] the Four Prohibitions.[86] The Four Prohibitions are the beginning of being broadened [in studying culture] and restrained [by means of rituals].[87]

[聖人與我同類者也. 衆人與聖同得此太極之理, 以爲性耳. 特爲氣禀所拘, 物欲所蔽, 有知愚賢不肖之等. 然其所受之本性則同矣. 是以, 覺者知吾 性之與堯舜同, 而求必得之, 如行者之尋家, 食者之求飽, 以期必至於聖. 夫聖之爲言, 不過大而化之之名而已. 孟子曰, 人皆可以爲堯舜. 凡人尙 可以爲堯舜, 況顏子亞聖之資乎. 雖然, 欲爲聖, 當先求顏子之所樂. 欲 求顏子之所樂, 當先學顏子之好學. 好學如之何. 四勿而已. 四勿, 當自 博約始.]

Yan Yuan was Confucius's most beloved student who allegedly had enjoyed the Way even in the midst of extreme poverty and destitution.[88] The Four Prohibitions refer to ritual precepts that Confucius recommended as the method to overcome one's self (*ji* 己), which Zhu Xi authoritatively reinterpreted in terms of the self-centeredness of human desires (*siyu* 私慾), when Yan Yuan inquired about becoming good. As Yunjidang saw it, at the heart of Yan Yuan's love of learning lay his moral desire to overcome the human heart–mind and preserve the heart–mind of the Way that contains the Heaven-decreed nature in its purest form. And this desire could only be realized through the ardent and painstaking practice of ritual propriety, which in eighteenth-century Korea was generally equated with the principle itself.[89]

In the quote above, Yunjidang's primary intent is to praise Yan Yuan, known in the Confucian tradition as one of the secondary sages. However, the motive behind her veneration of Yan Yuan is not so much to point out his extraordinariness or any special training that he received from Confucius. Rather, it is to draw attention to the fact, strongly affirmed by Neo-Confucian metaphysics, that *everyone* can become a sage like Yao and Shun. For Yunjidang, Yan Yuan was an ordinary man who, like others, was born with the original nature. What distinguished Yan Yuan from others was nothing more than his earnest aspiration to become good, which Yunjidang believes he was inherently capable of

---

[86] The Four Prohibitions are described in *Analects* 12.1: "Do not look unless it is in accordance with the rites; do not listen unless it is in accordance with the rites; do not speak unless it is in accordance with the rites; do not move unless it is in accordance with the rites."

[87] *Yunjidang yugo* 6b–7a (translation assisted by Philip J. Ivanhoe). Cf. *Analects* 6.27; 9.11.

[88] *Analects* 6.11. Also see *Analects* 6.7.

[89] For a similar rise of rituals (and ritual propriety) in China during the late Ming and early Qing periods, see Kai-Wing Chow, *The Rise of Confucian Ritualism in Late Imperial China* (Stanford, CA: Stanford University Press, 1994).

qua human being. What captivated Yunjidang is that Yan Yuan became a (secondary) sage by recovering his heart–mind of the Way through learning and moral self-cultivation, thereby letting his original nature shine forth without much hindrance from human desires.

Then, remarkably, Yunjidang brings this realization to the possibility of her own moral perfectibility, something that was almost inconceivable for women – even for elite women – in eighteenth-century Korea. For Yunjidang, the fact that Yan Yuan could become good through his unflagging moral desire to improve himself, despite his humble origins, was enough to give her an equally strong motivation to likewise aspire to become a sage.

> Why is it that we are unable to become like [such ancient sages as] Yao, Shun, the Duke of Zhou, and Confucius, despite the fact that human nature is absolutely good? It is because human desires have impaired our original nature. If we are able to eliminate such desires, Heavenly Principle [within us] will be naturally preserved and accordingly we can become sages such as Yao, Shun, the Duke of Zhou, and Confucius. Thus Yanzi said, "What kind of a person was Shun and what kind of a person am I? Only through practice, can I also become like him." Here "practice" means first clearly identifying the difference between the Heavenly Principle and human desires and sincerely practicing [what is guided by] the former.[90]
>
> [夫人性皆善, 而不能爲堯舜周孔者, 何也. 人欲害之也. 能制人欲, 則天理自存, 而我亦可以爲堯舜周孔矣. 故顏子之言曰, 舜何人也, 予何人也, 有爲者亦若是.有爲云者, 謂於天理人欲之分, 明辨而篤行之.]

It is worth noting that Yao, Shun, and the Duke of Zhou were all sages of Chinese antiquity, to whom Confucius showed his great admiration while refusing to allow himself to be called a sage.[91] Confucius also said, referring to sages, "those who are born with knowledge are the highest [class of human beings]."[92] Although, certainly, Confucius's expression of humility in declining to put himself in the league of ancient sages only makes his moral character all the more splendid, his remark could result in unintended consequences: It could make sagehood an unattainable ideal, accessible only by extraordinary individuals born with special talents.

In this regard, Zhu Xi's Neo-Confucian reinterpretation of Confucius's remarks must have been refreshing to Yunjidang, because he rendered as sages those who have fully realized their inborn nature or their heart–mind of the Way. Indeed, Zhu Xi's authoritative rereading of the *Analects* (and other Confucian classics) enabled Yunjidang to conclude that insomuch as all human

---

[90] *Yunjidang yugo* 50b (translation assisted by Philip J. Ivanhoe).
[91] *Analects* 7.34. Also see 7.20.   [92] *Analects* 16.9.

beings possess the same original nature bestowed by Heaven and have the innate moral potential to become a sage, those who have failed to become like a Yao and a Shun – the petty men in other words – could only blame themselves for letting their heart–minds of the Way be overpowered by their self-centered desires.[93] Thus, Yunjidang concludes,

> Suppose people are aware that the perfectly good nature of Yao and Shun is also within themselves and so they strenuously work on it, strengthening what they share with the sages while transforming what distinguishes them from the sages. Then, regardless of whether one's *qi* is clear or turbid, all can arrive at goodness by recovering the original state of one's nature. This is why it is said that [sages and people are] the same from the standpoint of their successful moral self-cultivation."[94]

As such, Yunjidang was strongly convinced that sagehood is a moral ideal open to anyone, including herself, and this conviction further led her to see herself not so much as a mere "woman" (k. *mu a puin* 無我婦人) as conventionally understood in Chosŏn society,[95] but as a *junzi*, a moral knight diligently and strenuously making her way toward sagehood. Yunjidang's commitment to the Neo-Confucian program of moral self-cultivation is most forcefully expressed in the following poem she composed:

> While a petty man finds life profitable,
> A *junzi* finds righteousness profitable.
> If it is difficult to have both [life and righteousness],
> I would rather take the latter.
> . . .
> Great is the will!
> Being the master of the myriad things
> Seven Emotions follow the right track [prescribed by the will]
> [And] all parts of the human body obey its command.
> If one is able to establish the will,
> Both practice and nature will be perfected.[96]

> [小人利生, 君子利義, 二者難兼, 維義是比. ... 大哉志兮, 萬事之領, 七情順軌, 百體從令, 能立厥志, 習與性成.]

Refusing to be a conventional woman who blindly follows society's rituals and norms, Yunjidang here declares herself to be a *junzi* (in the gender-neutral sense), wholeheartedly committed to the moral path of righteousness. She calls

---

[93] From this perspective, Peimin Ni reconstructs the Confucian account of dignity as moral achievement. See Peimin Ni, "Seek and You Will Find It; Let Go and You Will Lose It: Exploring a Confucian Approach to Human Dignity," *Dao* 13 (2014), pp. 174–198.

[94] *Yunjidag yugo* 32a (人能知堯舜至善之性, 亦在於我而力學之. 以充其同而變其殊, 則氣無清濁, 皆可至乎善, 而復其性之本然矣. 此所謂及其成功則一者也).

[95] *Yunjidang yugo* 51b.   [96] *Yunjidang yugo* 49a.

this unswerving commitment "the great will" and understands it as the master that commands human emotions and desires, generally called "Seven Emotions" by Neo-Confucians. Yunjidang believes that if she relentlessly and earnestly practices righteousness (and probably other virtues as well), she can arrive at the point of moral perfection where the distinction between practice and nature becomes pointless. For at the consummate stage of moral self-cultivation, ritual practice and the principle of ritual propriety within her nature would be perfectly harmonized.

2.3 Female Sagehood

At this point, it should be recalled that the second question of the Horak debate was whether sages and ordinary people possess the same heart–mind. Our discussion thus far clearly shows where Yunjidang stands on this question. Her moral universalism holds that there is no inherent difference between sages and ordinary people. What differentiates them is whether one has the will to overcome private desires and is able to preserve the Heavenly Principle within one's original nature through learning and ritual practice. In Yunjidang's view, no one should be regarded as lacking moral agency understood in this way, nor should anyone be prevented from developing it and achieving sage-hood. Even though the male participants in the Horak debate of her time were preoccupied with the question of whether, despite the differing endowments of *qi*, there can be this kind of moral subjectivity open to everyone, by "everyone" they generally meant *men* and the question that they grappled with was whether the ideal of sagehood was open to men of different natural endowments and, more controversially, of different social classes.

Now, when Yunjidang applied Neo-Confucian moral universalism to herself and explored the possibility of her own sagehood, a wholly new perspective opened which had never been anticipated by the key participants in the Horak debate. It was the question of female sagehood.

> Oh! When has Heaven ever produced a human being who is not benevolent? It is only because people's heart–minds are servants to their physical bodies that they settle into doing violence to [themselves] and throwing [themselves] away.[97] They then will say, "My endowment of *qi* is not fine; how could I presume to study the way of the sages and worthies?" Indecent and stupid, they act only for their own well-being and behave in ways that violate ritual propriety. Willingly, they will stoop to become the worst sort of thieves and never recognize how sad it is that they rot like grass and wood or how

---

[97] Cf. *Mencius* 4A10.

shameful it is that they are not much different from the birds and beasts. Ah! Those who are like this already are deeply mired in delusion; one cannot talk with them about benevolence. Truly their situation is as Confucius said, "In the end, what can one do with them?"[98] Ah! Though I am a woman, the nature I originally received was no different from that of a man. Though I am unable to study what Yan Yuan studied, I am completely earnest in sharing his aspiration to become a sage. And so, I have summarized what I have seen and written it down here to serve as a repository for my thoughts.[99]

[嗚呼. 天之生民何嘗不仁. 惟其心爲形役, 安於暴棄. 而乃曰, 我氣質不美, 豈敢學聖賢哉. 仳仳焉蠢蠢焉, 惟己是循, 惟非禮是行. 甘爲下品之賤, 而不復識其與草木同腐之爲可哀, 違禽獸不遠之爲可羞. 嗟夫, 若此者, 蔽痼已甚, 不可以語仁. 眞夫子所謂末如之何者也, 噫, 我雖婦人, 而所受之性, 則初無男女之殊. 縱不能學顏淵之所學, 而其慕聖之志則切. 故略叙所見而述此, 以寓意焉.]

In claiming that a woman can also share Yan Yuan's aspiration to become a sage, Yunjidang is not asserting that women must become like men by participating in their moral ideal. Nor is she merely declaring the possibility of female sagehood, that every woman can become a sage specific to her female identity, which is qualitatively different from that of men. What is central to Yunjidang is her belief that female sagehood is premised on the fundamental moral equality between men and women, not only because they are equally born with the Heaven-bestowed original nature,[100] but also because there is no qualitative difference between men and women in the quality of moral character one can possess after moral self-cultivation. Many scholars who are keen to present Yunjidang as a feminist thinker concentrate on her argument for the possibility of female sagehood and tend to take for granted that it is the natural corollary of her belief in moral equality between men and women.[101] But they are two different matters that are logically independent of each other, because one can still make an argument for female sagehood that is morally inferior to male sagehood. It is the way in which Yunjidang creates a philosophical connection between the two theses that

---

[98] *Analects* 15.16; cf. 9.24.

[99] *Yunjidang yugo* 44a–b (translation assisted by Philip J. Ivanhoe).

[100] Also see *Yunjidang yugo* 58a (男女, 雖曰異行, 而天命之性, 則未嘗不同).

[101] Kim Chae-im (김재임), "Yunjidang yugoe nat'anan yŏsŏng ŭisik koch'al (윤지당유고에 나타난 여성의식 고찰) [An Examination on the Feminist Consciousness in the *Bequeathed Writings of Im Yunjidang*]," *Hanmun kojŏn yŏn'gu* 10 (2005), pp. 215–256; Ku Min-chŏng (구민정), "Im yunjidangŭi chagi chŏngch'esŏngŭi kusŏnge taehayŏ (임윤지당의 자기 정체성의 구성에 대하여) [On the Construction of Im Yunjidang's Self-Identity]," *Inmunhak yŏn'gu* 29:2 (2019), pp. 27–49; Kim Sesŏria (김세서리아), "Im yunjidangŭi nonŏ ihae'e taehan yŏsŏng ch'ŏrakchŏk sŏngch'al (임윤지당의 논어 이해에 대한 여성철학적 성찰) [A Feminist Reflection on Im Yunjidang's Interpretation of the *Analects*]," *Han'guk yŏsŏng ch'ŏrak* 28 (2017), pp. 27–53.

marks her philosophical originality as a feminist thinker. Let me start with moral equality between men and women.

It should be reminded that Yunjidang's exploration of the Heaven-decreed nature, which she identified with the physical nature that every being is born with, was prompted by the third question of the Horak debate: whether the natures of human beings and nonhuman animals are identical. As we have seen, Yunjidang arrived at her unique philosophical conclusion, at the heart of which is the rejection of the metaphysical distinction between the original nature and the physical nature, through her equally creative reinterpretation of the Neo-Confucian theory of "Principle is one and its particularizations are many" from the perspective of the embodied nature (or physical nature) of each being or thing.

However, Yunjidang's metaphysical theory reveals some ambiguities. She argues that the natures of human beings and nonhuman animals (and nonliving things) are different because the notion of "the particularizations are many" informs both the distinctive endowments of qi and the particularized principle that is entwined with a specific endowment of qi – hence her refusal to see li and qi in binary terms. Implicit in her claim is that the notion of "the particularizations are many" can account for the different natures of the myriad things as *species* in the universe. This implies that human beings and nonhuman animals are distinguished as different species, if, for the sake of argument, we consider "nonhuman animals" as one general species. In any event, like other Neo-Confucian scholars of her time, Yunjidang's eminent concern was to demonstrate the difference between human nature and the nature(s) of nonhuman animals and other things, and not so much the differences between all distinct beings and things in the universe. Accordingly, she paid little attention to the distinctive individuality of each person or to the plurality of individual human beings, arguably one of the guiding concerns of Western moral and political philosophy.[102] As far as Yunjidang's metaphysical theory of li, qi, and human nature is concerned, the philosophical dyad that drove her philosophical reasoning was always humans (*ren* 人), on the one side, and nonhuman beings and things (*wu* 物), on the other. Like other Neo-Confucians, she was interested in the difference between human beings and nonhuman animals primarily as a virtue ethicist, that is, in order to

---

[102] Put differently, Yunjidang showed no interest in the value of human plurality of the kind that characterizes "the human condition" that Hannah Arendt famously attributes to ancient Greeks and the subsequent republican tradition of the West. For Arendt's valorization of human plurality, see Hannah Arendt, *The Human Condition* (Chicago, IL: University of Chicago Press, 1958).

explain why humans alone can experience moral growth and fully recover the Heaven-decreed nature.[103]

Therefore, as a metaphysician of human nature Yunjidang showed little interest in the distinction between men and women. She did not probe such questions as how humans are differentiated into men and women from the perspective of Neo-Confucian cosmology of *li* and *qi*, whether men and women should be understood as two different (human) species, and how the biological differences between men and women should be understood in comparison with the difference between human beings and nonhuman animals. However, now that Yunjidang revisits her otherwise universal moral individualism and the Confucian theory of moral self-cultivation with special focus on her identity as a woman, she realizes, though implicitly, that there is a problem with her general interest in human beings or with her lack of a metaphysical discussion on the distinction between men and women. On the one hand, insomuch as Yunjidang acknowledges the obvious biological differences between men and women, her metaphysical argument of the particularized and embodied nature containing a distinctive principle must apply to the distinction between men and women. On the other hand, this distinction must not undermine the commonality that binds men and women as single human species, equally capable of moral self-development, and thus distinguished from nonhuman animals and other things whose turbid and imbalanced endowments of *qi* do not allow for their moral development. Yunjidang's philosophical question, then, comes down to that of how to account for women's particularized and embodied nature in light of the universal theory of Confucian moral self-cultivation.

Unfortunately, Yunjidang left no organized philosophical account on this matter. But this does not mean that she did not grapple with this question philosophically. It only means that a careful reconstruction of her philosophical argument is necessary in order to understand how she builds a theoretical connection between the idea of particularized and embodied human nature with a distinctive *li* (and *qi*) and her universalist ethics of self-cultivation and moral individualism.[104] In this regard, the following statement that Im Chŏngju attributes to his sister provides an important clue:

---

[103] Indeed, some contemporary Confucian scholars understand Zhu Xi's moral program in terms of virtue ethics. See Stephen C. Angle, *Sagehood: The Contemporary Significance of Neo-Confucian Philosophy* (New York: Oxford University Press, 2009); Yat-hung Leung, "Zhu Xi and the Debate between Virtue Ethicists and Situationists: Virtue Cultivation as a Possible, Practical, and Necessary Enterprise," in *Dao Companion to Zhu Xi's Philosophy*, ed. Kai-chiu Ng and Yong Huang (Dordrecht: Springer, 2020), pp. 895–927.

[104] On the idea of moral individualism in the (Neo-)Confucian tradition, see Wm. Theodore de Bary, *The Liberal Tradition in China* (New York: Columbia University Press, 1983).

The way of a man is being strong; the way of a woman is being gentle. Each thing and being has its own principle. That is why the tasks of the female sage Tai Si 太姒 [King Wen's wife] and the sage[-king] Wen were different. Their differences are different manifestations [of the same principle]. They are the same in the sense that both fulfilled the original nature, which represents the oneness of the principle. If King Wen had been a female and Tai Si a male, they would have naturally fulfilled their [exchanged] roles. Therefore, if a woman does not wish to be like Tai Si and Tai Ren 太任 [King Wen's mother], it would amount to self-injury and self-abandonment.[105]

[乾健坤順, 各有其則. 聖姒聖文, 所行異宜者, 分之殊也. 盡性則同者, 理之一也. 易地則皆然. 然則婦人而不以任姒自期者, 皆自棄也.]

Trusting that Yunjidang indeed stated this, three points can be gleaned. First, although men and women both belong to the human species, they are distinguished in the sense that men and women are born with distinctive principles that constitute distinctive natures. Second, the fact that men and women are born with distinctive principles that are at once metaphysical and moral entails that the specific moral characteristics that are expected of men and women are accordingly different. More specifically, the way of a man is modeled after Heaven, which is strong, while the way of a woman is modeled after Earth, which is gentle. When Yunjidang says that "[human beings can] model themselves after the Way of Heaven and Earth and be harmonized with the virtue of them,"[106] she seems to have in mind that men and women should, *respectively,* embody the virtues of Heaven and Earth, and when they each succeed in doing so they can *together* form oneness with the Way of Heaven and Earth. In short, men and women are different but they are complementary to each other. Third, even though the specific moral characteristics that are expected of men and women are different, and thus the social roles that they are supposed to carry out also differ, there is no qualitative difference in the moral characters that a man and a woman can attain after moral self-cultivation. To explicate this last point, Yunjidang draws attention to the cases of King Wen and Tai Si, King Wen's virtuous wife, and interprets their virtues in reference to Neo-Confucian metaphysics.

As noted earlier, King Wen was the founder of the Zhou dynasty, one of the three dynasties of the Chinese antiquity that Confucius admired the most. Tai Si, his wife, faithfully followed in the footsteps of Tai Ren, her mother-in-law, and excellently fulfilled her "wifely virtues," as best evidenced by the fact that she gave birth to her husband's male heir, King Wu, and raised him well.[107] In Yunjidang's view, the successful founding of the Zhou dynasty was possible

---

[105] *Yunjidang yugo* 81a.   [106] *Yunjidang yugo* 25b ([人]以其能體天地之道, 而與之合其德也.).
[107] On Tai Si and Tai Ren, see Goldin, "The View of Women in Early Confucianism," pp. 136–145.

because King Wen and Tai Si each played their specific roles as a man (father/ king) and as a woman (mother/wife). Following Hye-Kyung Kim, we may find here what can be called "gender essentialism," which consists of the following three propositions: (1) members of a gender share essential characteristics; (2) the shared characteristics of different genders differ; and (3) the different essential traits of different genders are rooted in fixed biological differences, especially those having to do with sex.[108]

What is interesting is that contrary to most modern feminists, Yunjidang sees no conflict between gender essentialism and moral equality between men and women. Once again, the key to understanding Yunjidang's seemingly counter-intuitive position lies in her interpretation of the Neo-Confucian theory of "Principle is one and its particularizations are many." It is important to note that Yunjidang does not stop with the statement that King Wen and Tai Si fulfilled the original nature, which could possibly imply moral inequality between men and women unless it is explicitly denied that there is a qualitative difference between men and women in their original natures. In fact, Yunjidang believed that there are fundamental moral differences between human beings and nonhuman animals because the latter's original nature is embodied in the *qi* that is turbid and imbalanced, making their moral improvement impossible or very difficult. Now, she explicates King Wen's and Tai Si's fulfillment of the original nature from the standpoint of the oneness of the principle. Otherwise stated, she notes no qualitative difference in the original natures of King Wen and Tai Si as they are equally regulated by the same Heaven-given principle. Moreover, for Yunjidang the oneness of the principle vindicates the equal quality of moral achievements that King Wen and Tai Si each attained. The differences between them in their moral characteristics and the specific gendered social roles they are expected to fulfill represent the distinct forms of particularization of the same moral principle.

The upshot of Yunjidang's reconstructed argument can be recapitulated as follows. First, the original natures of human beings and nonhuman animals (and other things in the universe) are not identical. Second, human beings share the same original nature. Third, as human beings, men and women possess the same original nature in the sense that they possess the same innate capacity to realize moral virtues such as benevolence, righteousness, ritual propriety, wisdom, and trustworthiness. Fourth, given the differing endowments of *qi* that men and women each possess (strong versus gentle), their original natures, though morally equal, are differently constituted in such a way that men can actualize

---

[108] Hye-Kyung Kim, "Yunjidang's Feminism and Gender Equality," *Asian Philosophy* 31:2 (2021), pp. 143–159 (p. 148).

their inborn strength and women their inborn gentleness. Fifth and finally, there are specific gendered social roles for men and women, enabling them to properly actualize their inborn strength or gentleness. Yunjidang's philosophical genius is that she understands gender essentialism (i.e., male = strong versus female = gentle) and moral capacity to realize cardinal human virtues – the cultivation of which enables human beings to attain sagehood – as mutually independent. That is, the fact that a woman is supposed to carry out social roles that are specific to her distinctive female original nature does not prevent her from achieving the same moral ideal (i.e., sagehood) to which her male counterpart also aspires. It is for this reason that Yunjidang is convinced that if King Wen had been a woman and Tai Si a man, they would have naturally fulfilled their exchanged roles.[109]

Thus understood, it is obvious that Yunjidang's core concern is far from reinforcing her metaphysical belief in gender essentialism. The point she is trying to make is twofold: (1) men and women are morally equal and (2) there is no moral hierarchy between male sagehood and female sagehood. In Yunjidang's view, that women are expected to fulfill female virtues should be no excuse for self-injury and self-abandonment, because there is no indignity in being a woman or carrying out virtues that are specific to her Heaven-given identity as a woman. A woman becomes undignified when she abandons her commitment to cultivate herself morally, that is, when she does not wish to be like Tai Si or Tai Ren anymore. To put this in Neo-Confucian terms, the failure to fulfill (what we now consider to be) gendered virtues is directly tantamount to injuring one's heart–mind of the Way. And succumbing to one's human heart–mind or human desires is nothing more than relegating oneself to the state of a beast. As Yunjidang saw it, self-abandonment of this sort is the moral challenge equally faced by ordinary men and women. Indeed, it is this very problem that Yan Yuan, Yunjidang's moral hero, wrestled with and overcame.

For Yunjidang, therefore, it would be a grave mistake to believe that social roles prescribed for men and women are mere social constructions that can be subject to radical deconstruction by human agency encumbered by nothing including Heaven or the Heavenly Principle. Yunjidang would find it equally wrong to regard gendered social roles simply as the tool of social control by which to maintain male hegemony over women. As discussed earlier, Yunjidang, like other Neo-Confucians of her time, understood ritually sanctioned social roles as the concrete expression of the universal moral principle of

---

[109] As Hye-Kyung Kim rightly notes (ibid., p. 154), in making this argument, Yunjidang seems to have in mind *Mencius* 4B29 where Mencius says, "Yu, Ji, and Yan Hui [another name for Yan Yuan] were at one in the Way. ... Were Yu and Ji and Master Yan to have changed places, each would have acted in the same way."

ritual propriety that equally regulates the conduct of men and women, albeit through different ritual forms. As such, her moral ideal of female sagehood is intelligible only against this Neo-Confucian philosophical backdrop.

3 Im Yunjidang and Confucian Feminism

3.1 The Contemporary Debate

This leaves us with perhaps the most controversial question regarding Im Yunjidang. Can we call Yunjidang a feminist thinker?

The feminist interpreters of Yunjidang – let us call them "the Enthusiasts" – tend to present her as a critic of social discrimination against women, especially their exclusion from more advanced Confucian education in public institutions, which was accessible only to male members of the *yangban* class.[110] The evidence that they often draw attention to is Yunjidang's short biography of Lady Han from Ch'ŏngju, who married a man from a prominent *yangban* family but died young. In the biography, Yunjidang praises Lady Han for being a woman with remarkable wisdom and of excellent moral conduct who corrected her husband's preoccupation with worldly reputation through wise, yet gentle, admonishment and eventually helped him become an accomplished Confucian scholar. As modern scholars point out, while praising Lady Han's remarkable talent and virtue (wifely virtues, to be more precise), Yunjidang deeply lamented that her father blindly adhered to the conventional social practice of the time and did not arrange a proper education for his daughter with Confucian classics and historical texts, leaving her to study them by herself.[111] According to Pak Hyŏn-suk, Yunjidang's criticism of Lady Han's father reveals her implicit acknowledgment of women's *right* to equal (public) education, which was unjustly denied to them. Pak goes further and argues that Yunjidang's conviction that men and women are born with the same Heaven-given nature naturally entails her critical stance toward Chosŏn's institutional structures which did not grant women the opportunity to have an education equal with men – against Confucianism's original egalitarian spirit.[112]

---

[110] Throughout the Chosŏn dynasty, male commoners were able to attend various sorts of private village schools called *sŏdang* (k. 書堂) where they could learn Chinese characters and receive elementary Confucian education. Female commoners were excluded even from these unofficial education settings, which were often run by retired Confucian scholars or old village gurus. See Chŏng Sun-wu (정순우), *Sŏdangŭi sahoesa* (서당의 사회사) [*The Sociology of the Local Private Village School*] (Seoul: T'aehaksa, 2012).

[111] *Yunjidang yugo* 1b.

[112] Pak Hyŏn-suk (박현숙), "Im yunjidangnon (임윤지당론) [A Study on Im Yunjidang]," *Yŏsŏng munhakyŏn'gu* 9 (2003), pp. 131–156 (pp. 136–137). See also Kim, "Yunjidang yugoe nat'anan yŏsŏng ŭisik koch'al," p. 242.

Yi Hye-chin's interpretation of Yunjidang is more radical. On Yi's account, Yunjidang was the Korean equivalent of Mary Wollstonecraft (1759–97), a feminist who espoused women's moral subjectivity as equal to that of men and attempted to subvert late Chosŏn's heavily androcentric and gendered social order which was deeply sexist and discriminatory. In short, according to Yi, there is essentially no difference between Yunjidang and modern liberal feminists who struggled to emancipate women from the yokes of patriarchal social customs and practices.[113] Although she finds Yi Hye-chin's feminist reading of Yunjidang too subversive, Mun Chi-yŏng, too, believes that the comparison between Yunjidang and Wollstonecraft is meaningful in the sense that both women were frustrated by existing social norms and institutional practices that discriminated against women, and this painful recognition led them to become strong advocates of equal opportunity to education. Mun, however, notes an important difference between Yunjidang and Wollstonecraft: While Wollstonecraft espoused a more radical social and political reform in order to make fundamental changes with regard to women's civil, economic, and political rights, Yunjidang's feminism did not develop into an advocacy of women's right to political participation and equal citizenship. Mun speculates that Yunjidang's lack of interest in more radical social reform might have to do with the distinctive understanding of "the political" in the Confucian tradition,[114] to which I will return shortly.

Scholars who cast doubt on the feminist interpretation of Yunjidang – let us call them "the Skeptics" – find fault with the Enthusiasts for failing to take Yunjidang's intellectual and political contexts seriously, although few of them necessarily deny the fact that she advanced a novel Neo-Confucian justification for moral equality between men and women. Yi Suk-in, for instance, asserts that Yunjidang hardly succeeded in constructing, let alone vindicating, independent female identity.[115] As Yi sees it, it was far from Yunjidang's most eminent concern to develop a distinctive female (moral, social, and political) identity

---

[113] Yi Hye-chin (이해진), "'Yŏsŏng'esŏ 'in'ganŭro, chuch'erŭl hyanghan yŏlmang: Im yunji-dang'gwa ulstonkraeptŭ pigyo yŏn'gu ('여성'에서 '인간'으로, 주체를 향한 열망: 임윤지당과 울스턴크래프트 비교 연구) [From Woman to Human, the Passion toward a Moral Subject: A Comparative Study on Im Yunjidang and Wollstonecraft]," *Han'guk yŏsŏnghak* 30:2 (2014), pp. 89–125.

[114] Mun Chi-yŏng (문지영), "'Yŏsŏng ch'abyŏre taehan tong sŏyangŭi insikkwa tojŏn: Im yunji-danggwa ulstonkraeptŭrŭl chungsimŭro ('여성차별'에 대한 동서양의 인식과 도전: 임윤지당과 울스턴크래프트를 중심으로) [An Understanding of and Challenge to 'Discrimination against Women' in East and West: Focusing on Im Yunjidang and Wollstonecraft]," *Han'guk chŏngch'ihak hoebo* 50:1 (2016), pp. 23–49.

[115] See also Yu Yŏng-hŭi (유영희), "Im yunjidangŭi sŏngni ch'ŏrakkwa suhaengnon (임윤지당의 성리 철학과 수행론) [Im Yunjidang's Neo-Confucian Philosophy and Her Account of Moral Self-Cultivation]," *Han'guk sasanggwa munhwa* 29 (2005), pp. 231–261.

because she single-mindedly pursued the ideal of *junzi*, essentially, according to Yi, the male Confucian moral ideal, and it was the "learning to become a *junzi*" (k. *kunjahak* 君子學) that motivated, as well as shaped, both her scholarship and her moral conduct during her entire life. Therefore, Yi continues, what we find in Yunjidang's lifelong struggle to become a *junzi* is not so much the development of female subjectivity but the tension between her everyday female identity, which she embraced wholeheartedly, and her aspiration toward male moral subjectivity.[116]

Of note is that Yi Suk-in explains this tension or the inappropriateness of understanding Yunjidang as a feminist thinker from a broader structural perspective. Yi's starting point is the "Small China" ideology that dominated the minds of the *yangban* aristocratic class who were soaked in Neo-Confucianism after the collapse of the Ming empire in China. Yi argues that envisioning Chosŏn as an authentic heir to the Confucian civilization that had originated in China, Chosŏn's Neo-Confucian ruling elites, both men and women, were completely immersed in Sinocentric cultural universalism, of which Chosŏn had now become the center, and they associated their cultural and moral identity directly with their Chinese Confucian heroes. Central to Yi's argument is that the deepening of Confucian patriarchy in late Chosŏn society was the natural corollary of elite Koreans' immersion in Sinocentric universalism, which was premised on the irrevocable moral hierarchies between lord and subject, between father and son, and between men and women. According to Yi, just as Chosŏn, once at the periphery of Sinocentric global order, transformed itself into the center of that order by actively embracing Sinocentric Confucian moral discourse comprising righteousness and ritual propriety, so elite Korean women, including Yunjidang, eagerly internalized the androcentric knowledge system and patriarchal social norms and did not question the dominant knowledge system itself that was heavily gendered and discriminatory. Thus, Yi Suk-in concludes that, as a woman philosopher, Yunjidang maneuvered herself within the system of patriarchal knowledge, of which the moral ideals of Tai Si, Tai Ren, and female sagehood were all integral parts, only to reinforce the androcentric social order.[117]

In the same vein, though from a slightly different angle, Kim Youngmin is skeptical that Yunjidang wished to go beyond the inner chambers or support anything other than Chosŏn's existing Neo-Confucian moral norms and social practices. Kim, who is not convinced of any novelty in Yunjidang's

---

[116] Yi Suk-in (이숙인), "Chosŏnsidae yŏsŏng chisigŭi sŏngkkyŏkkwa kŭ kusŏng wŏlli (조선시대 여성 지식의 성격과 그 구성원리) [The Nature of Women's Knowledge and Its Constitutive Principle during the Chosŏn Period]," *Tongyang ch'ŏrak* 33 (2005), pp. 77–104 (pp. 90–91).

[117] Ibid., pp. 92–99.

philosophical thought, even asks whether it is plausible to interpret her as someone who self-consciously intended to "demonstrate" moral and intellectual equality between men and women. Kim claims that since Yunjidang lived in a world where philosophical originality was not valued as the (most important) standard for learning, our focus should be on the "performative" significance of her engagement in Neo-Confucian philosophy and ethics as a woman.[118] What was this performative significance, then, which Kim argues has nothing to do with any interest in sociopolitical reforms,' that would have improved women's social, economic, and political conditions? According to Kim, the key to understanding Yunjidang's life and philosophical work is her desire to become an active agent of rituals that defined her everyday life. That is, her realization that everyone, regardless of gender, possesses the same principle (or pattern, as Kim translates *li*) that unites all beings and things in the moral universe into metaphysical oneness led her to believe that one's self-transformation is directly connected with the transformation of the world itself. Kim, then, concludes as follows:

> This kind of unique vision of the self's relation to the world [via *li*] allowed the Chinese literati in [the] late imperial period and the Korean *yangban* in late Chosŏn to feel socially responsible while they remain in local society without being able to hold office. . . . By the same token, . . . Im Yunjidang and Kang Chŏngildang were able to feel socially responsible even when they remained in the inner chambers. In fact, they did not have to leave the domestic realm to attain sociopolitical significance, insofar as they could appropriate the whole world in the realm of the self. In a sense, the inner chamber was a functional equivalent of local society.[119]

According to Kim's interpretation, therefore, it hardly mattered to Yunjidang whether the moral agent in question was a man or a woman; what mattered most to her was whether one was earnestly committed to moral self-transformation through ritual practice and, thereby, could attain the unity between herself and the whole moral universe through the all-encompassing moral principle within herself.[120]

---

[118] Youngmin Kim, "Neo-Confucianism as Free-Floating Resource: Im Yunjidang and Kang Chŏngildang as Two Female Neo-Confucian Philosophers in Late Chosŏn," in *Women and Confucianism in Chosŏn Korea*, eds. Kim and Pettid, pp. 71–88.

[119] Ibid., p. 84.

[120] In making this argument, Kim Youngmin criticizes Kim Hyŏn who argues that Yunjidang's argument for moral equality between men and women could be understood as the consequence of the religionization of Neo-Confucianism in late Chosŏn society, which encouraged the Neo-Confucians of the time to concentrate mainly on one's inner world; see Kim Hyŏn (김현), "Sŏngnihakchŏk kach'igwanŭi hwaksan'gwa yŏsŏng (성리학적 가치관의 확산과 여성) [The Spread of Neo-Confucian Values and Women]," *Minjok munhwa yŏn'gu* 41 (2004), pp. 455–488. It is unclear, however, precisely what Kim Youngmin takes issue with because Kim Hyŏn

Although Kim does not make this explicit, Yunjidang's lack of interest in the radical transformation of Chosŏn into a more egalitarian society where women enjoy equal moral standing and rights, boils down, in the end, to Neo-Confucianism's complex understanding of "publicness" (*gong* 公). According to this concept, all social realms, including the family and local communities, hold moral value and public meaning to such an extent that it makes them coeval to the state and even to the whole world in their moral significance.[121] Or, as Mun Chi-yŏng puts it, Yunjidang's unifying understanding of the self and the world can be explained by the Neo-Confucian conception of "the political" or "the Public Way" (*gongdao* 公道), which stands on the opposite side to the privateness of human desires. Insofar as one engages in moral practice with a view to preserving one's heart–mind of the Way, one should be regarded as employed in public service in the most profound sense.[122]

Yet, the most forceful criticism of the feminist interpretation of Yunjidang comes from contemporary feminist scholars who find gender essentialism inherently incompatible with the moral ideal that feminism stands for. Among others, Kang Nam-sun criticizes any attempt to build a mutually constitutive relationship between Confucianism and feminism as more dangerous than outright gender discrimination. Although she does not directly engage with Yunjidang or contemporary scholars who interpret her as a feminist (i.e., the Enthusiasts), she makes it abundantly clear that unless the thinker in question actively and self-consciously challenges gendered social norms and practices and advocates women's total emancipation from an androcentric and patriarchal order, it is impossible to call him or her a feminist. The following statement, though rather lengthy, contains Kang's core argument which applies with equal force to the feminist interpretations of Yunjidang as well:

---

does not claim that the religionization of Korean Neo-Confucianism turned one completely away from the question of social and political responsibility. Kim Hyŏn's central argument is that Yunjidang's Neo-Confucianism can be understood in terms of religious practice, and this argument is compatible with Kim Youngmin's own interpretation of Yunjidang as immersed in the unity between self and world. For a similar, religious interpretation of Yunjidang's Neo-Confucian philosophy and ritual practice, see Yi Ŭn-sŏn (이은선), *Irŏbŏrin ch'owŏrŭl ch'ajasŏ: Han'guk yugyoŭi chonggyojŏk sŏngch'algwa yŏsŏngjuŭi* (잃어버린 초월을 찾아서: 한국 유교의 종교적 성찰과 여성주의) [*In Search of Lost Transcendence: Religious Reflexivity and Feminism in Korean Confucianism*] (Seoul: Monsinŭn saramdŭl, 2009), pp. 101–133.

[121] On the multidimensional meanings of publicness in Neo-Confucianism, see Seung-Hwan Lee, "The Concept of *Gong* in Traditional Korea and Its Modern Transformations," *Korea Journal* 43 (2003), pp. 137–163.

[122] This idea harkens all the way back to Confucius who stated, "The *Book of History* says, 'Oh! Simply by being a good son and friendly to his brothers a man can exert an influence upon government.' In so doing a man is, in fact, taking part in government. How can there be any question of his having actively to 'take part in government'?" (*Analects* 2.21).

What is certain is that any feminist who takes seriously women's freedom and equality and democratic values would find Confucian relationalism [unacceptable]. For at the heart of Confucian relationalism lies androcentric hierarchical relationships between men and women, between legitimate and illegitimate children, between husband and wife, between son and daughter, and between *yangban* and commoner, which are fundamentally at odds with the individualistic conception of human beings. Confucian relationalism is likely to support pseudo-egalitarianism that holds that men and women are *equal but different*; but it ultimately fails to provide [from within] an alternative principle like "equal relationalism," which constitutes the core of feminism [understood as a political theory and movement] that explores equality and justice in each and every sphere of human life, encompassing social, political, economic, religious, and cultural domains. Moreover, I cannot but remain deeply skeptical that Confucianism can ever be compatible with feminism, one of the most radical and regime-transformative political movements in human history in that [first] Confucianism never regarded the underprivileged as its primary audience and that [second] it explains the moral principles, which aim to preserve the existing regime rather than to challenge it, in terms of cosmological principles.[123]

What can we make of this debate? Since the question of whether Yunjidang can be reasonably called a Confucian feminist depends, in important part, on whether something like "Confucian feminism" is possible, let me start with Kang Nam-sun's general skepticism toward Confucian feminism and proceed to discuss why views that question the feminist character of Yunjidang's Neo-Confucian philosophy are problematic.

3.2 The Stage Approach to Feminism

I agree that there is always the possibility that Confucian feminism as a philosophical concept can be exploited to reinforce the moral and political hierarchy between men and women that has long been taken for granted in the Confucian tradition. I also agree that unless Confucian feminism shows us a way toward egalitarian relationality, its moral value would be difficult to appreciate. However, it is unclear from Kang's statement (and her entire essay) if her intention is to point to the possible exploitation of the otherwise philosophically sound concept or the impossibility of the concept itself as a normative guide. If Kang's real concern is with the second question, why does she cast doubt on the effort to develop a version of Confucianism that

---

[123] Kang Nam-sun (강남순), "Yugyowa p'eminisŭm: Kŭ pulganŭnghan manname taehayŏ (유교와 페미니즘: 그 불가능한 만남에 대하여) [Confucianism and Feminism: On Their Impossible Rendezvous]," in *Yugyuwa p'eminisŭm* (유교와 페미니즘) [*Confucianism and Feminism*], ed. Han'guk yugyo hakhoe (한국유교학회) (Seoul: Ch'ŏrakkwa hyŏnsilsa, 2001), pp. 271–282 (pp. 277–278) (translation is mine and emphasis is in the original).

upholds women's equal moral and political standing with men? Why should a particular historical form of Confucianism as it unfolded in premodern Korea prevent one from reinventing it into a democratic and feminist Confucianism? A comparison with "Confucian democracy" would be helpful here, which Samuel Huntington dismissively called "a contradiction in terms."[124]

Huntington's core argument is that Confucian values that valorize harmony and stability are fundamentally at odds with the minimal threshold of democracy marked by "equitable and open competition for votes between political parties with an absence of minimal levels of governmental harassment or restriction of opposition groups."[125] Thirty years after Huntington's provocative statement, there are few scholars who subscribe to his impossibility thesis. First, his claim has proven to be empirically false in that Confucian societies like South Korea and Taiwan successfully democratized their regimes without forfeiting their Confucian societal culture or, more accurately, by negotiating their traditional Confucian values with democratic principles, rights, and institutions.[126] Second, Huntington's claim is problematic in a philosophical sense as well. His underlying assumption is that "democracy" must invariably mean a Western-style liberal democracy and an argument for any form of "nonliberal democracy" should accordingly be held in doubt. Yet, in the past two decades, many scholars in East Asia and beyond have vigorously explored various normatively appealing accounts of Confucian democracy as an alternative to Western-style liberal democracy – a nonliberal democracy that is robustly democratic and progressive while maintaining key Confucian characteristics.[127] Confucian democrats consider Huntington's claim to be a liberal presumption.

The problem with Kang's argument is that she repeats the same mistake that Huntington and others have made. She takes for granted that the values of freedom and equality on which feminism is predicated presuppose (Western) modern individuality and any deviation from this foundational premise renders it unfeminist, or worse, anti-feminist. Like Huntington who

---

[124] Samuel P. Huntington, *The Third Wave: Democratization in the Late Twentieth Century* (Norman: University of Oklahoma Press, 1991), p. 307.

[125] Ibid., p. 305.

[126] See Geir Helgesen, *Democracy and Authority in Korea: The Cultural Dimension in Korean Politics* (Richmond, UK: Curzon, 1998); Joel Fetzer and J. Christopher Soper, *Confucianism, Democratization, and Human Rights in Taiwan* (Lanham, MD: Lexington Books, 2013).

[127] Brook A. Ackerly, "Is Liberalism the Only Way toward Democracy? Confucianism and Democracy," *Political Theory* 33 (2005), pp. 547–576; Stephen C. Angle, *Contemporary Confucian Political Philosophy* (Cambridge: Polity: 2012); Sungmoon Kim, *Confucian Democracy in East Asia: Theory and Practice* (New York: Cambridge University Press, 2014); Sor-hoon Tan, *Confucian Democracy: A Deweyan Reconstruction* (Albany: State University of New York Press, 2004).

believed that Confucian democracy is nothing more than a democracy dis-figured, Kang seems to believe that Confucian feminism is a pseudo-feminism because it does not actively challenge the Confucian way of life that, in her view, unjustly subjects women to patriarchal social and political hierarchy. Implicit in Kang's skepticism toward the happy congruence between Confucianism and feminism is the pessimism that there can be no Confucian feminism because, once decoupled from its androcentric and patriarchal core, Confucian feminism loses its Confucian essence, making the feminism in question un-Confucian. Ultimately, Kang's reasoning leads to the conclusion that Confucian feminism is practically impossible.

Like democracy, however, feminism can take many forms, as long as it meets the following minimal definition: It is *a philosophical doctrine that postulates equality between men and women with an explicit commitment to improve women's moral and material well-being*. Furthermore, we can approach femin-ism thus defined in terms of several stages and in a way that is intelligible to women themselves situated in a specific cultural and philosophical tradition. In this "stage approach" to feminism, as I am developing it here, the inchoate form of feminism begins with critical reflections on women's moral status, motivated from within the given cultural and philosophical tradition. In the next stage, it develops into a philosophical justification of moral equality between men and women as well as women's reflexive moral agency in reference to the best knowledge available in the specific historical time and cultural space. In the final stage, institutional changes are explored with a view to ensuring women's equal standing relative to men. The most salient advantage of this stage approach to feminism, which is also culturally sensitive, is that it does not posit the monolithic, anti-perfectionist, and culture-transcending ideal of women's moral agency. Its additional appeal is that it does not commit the fallacy of presentism, the mistake of imposing present moral standards on the past. For it pays close attention to the philosophical mechanism by which moral equality between men and women is (or was) understood and justified from within the given cultural tradition, especially by women themselves, as well as the specific mode of institutional change that such justification recommends, tacitly or explicitly.

How does this stage approach to feminism apply to Confucianism? Or how can we understand Confucian feminism from the standpoint of the stage approach? As I mentioned in the Introduction, albeit briefly, Confucianism is a form of virtue ethics, and in the mainstream Mencian tradition, from which the Neo-Confucian Learning of Principle originated, any account of Confucian feminism should be grounded in the following propositions, though they hardly exhaust all philosophical tenets of Mencian Confucianism:

(1) Human nature is good in the sense of possessing moral sentiments that incline one toward goodness.

(2) Human flourishing lies in cultivating innate moral sentiments, thereby attaining formidable moral character, the culmination of which is sagehood.

(3) Well-being is understood in terms of both moral flourishing, as expressed in (2), and material sufficiency that enables one to steadily engage in moral self-cultivation.

(4) The *telos* of the state lies in protecting and promoting the well-being of the people.

(5) Protection and promotion of well-being is the good that should be equitably (*jun* 균) available for every person qua human being.[128]

(6) Social norms and/or institutional structures that stand in the way of the equitable protection and promotion of the well-being of the people must be reformed to ensure their foundational moral equality.[129]

The first stage of Confucian feminism begins with evaluating the core propositions of (Mencian) Confucianism from the perspective of a woman – whether she is fully included in this moral program. When it is found that Confucianism, both as a philosophical tradition as well as a cultural one, fails to meet its own ideal from the perspective of a woman, the next stage of Confucian feminism calls, first, for a critical investigation of this failure – whether historically contingent or integral to the tradition itself – and second, for a philosophical justification of women's moral agency based on moral equality between men and women. What is important here is that this justification must be consistent with Confucianism's core propositions, and an effort to meet this requirement of internal consistency does not necessarily preclude a creative reinterpretation of the tradition itself. The final stage, insofar as Confucian feminism is a political vision, is an exploration of institutional change, as recommended by philosophical investigation of the problems in question.

By "institutional change," however, I do not mean something like a total revolution or the draconian overhaul of existing institutional structures of the sorts that anticipate what contemporary feminists regard as acceptable. It must be something that can be reasonably and realistically pursued by women themselves in their struggle to improve both external conditions and social perceptions that have thus far prohibited them from protecting and promoting

---

[128] See *Analects* 16.1.

[129] On the fundamental moral equality among human beings in Mencian Confucianism, see Irene Bloom, "Mencian Confucianism and Human Rights," in *Confucianism and Human Rights*, eds. Wm. Theodore de Bary and Tu Weiming (New York: Columbia University Press, 1998), pp. 94–116.

their moral and material well-being. Introducing the constitutional protection of equal civil and political rights could be one way to embark upon institutional change toward this end, but the institutional change motivated by Confucian feminism does not have to rely on rights-protecting institutions *if* alternative Confucian institutional arrangements can be found that equally or better serve the well-being of men and women. Unfortunately, Kang's sweeping dismissal of the possibility of Confucian feminism, which is singularly based on the historical Confucianism that unfolded in Korea, does not do justice to an effort to transform the tradition from within. Moreover, Kang's strong skepticism does not seem to be able to come to terms with female Confucian philosophers like Im Yunjidang who critically recast the Confucian tradition from a rigorous philosophical standpoint and found the meaning of her life within that tradition by reformulating the related philosophical postulates of the original nature of women, their moral well-being, and their moral agency.

How about more moderate skeptics such as Yi Suk-in and Kim Youngmin? Is their skepticism plausible from the standpoint of the stage approach to feminism? More importantly, is their interpretation of Yunjidang's philosophical ideas reasonable?

No doubt, it is important to understand a thinker's philosophical ideas against the backdrop of the broad intellectual and political contexts in which she found herself, and that is exactly what has guided this Element as well. That being said, taking the context seriously is one thing and collapsing the thinker's philosophical ideas to the context is another. Certainly, Yi Suk-in is right to point out that the deepening of the Small China ideology among members of the *yangban* class since the seventeenth century facilitated their internalization of hierarchical norms that used to undergird the Sinocentric Confucian civilization and govern the relationship between Ming China and Chosŏn, reshaping the relationship between men and women correspondingly in a rigidly hierarchical fashion. This, however, does not make Yunjidang one of those *yangban* aristocrats who uncritically reproduced hierarchical and gendered norms in their daily ritual practices, failing to "take issue with the knowledge system itself that marginalized and excluded women."[130]

As many Enthusiasts rightly note, Yunjidang was clearly aware of the tension between women's exclusion from a wider range of Confucian education in late Chosŏn society and the inclusionary moral ideal of Confucianism; this critical reflection led her to lament the reality that had prevented her from accessing the sort of education that was available to Yan Yuan (or any male student of Confucianism). And it is in this very spirit that she found fault with Lady

---

[130] Yi, "Chosŏnsidae yŏsŏng chisigŭi sŏngkkyŏk," p. 97.

Han's father for blindly following the patriarchal social practices of the time that denied women education beyond elementary Confucian studies aimed at the inculcation of female virtues. More importantly, it does serious injustice to Yunjidang to claim that her subscription to the Small China ideology drove her to idolize Chinese female sages such as Tai Ren and Tai Si who, after all, were nothing more than exemplars of gendered female virtues. What is critically lacking in Yi Suk-in's study of Yunjidang (and Kang Chŏngildang) is a detailed philosophical analysis of the way in which Yunjidang reappraised female virtues as the vehicle toward female sagehood – that is morally equal to male sagehood. All in all, Yi Suk-in's structural approach is unable to appreciate the fact that Yunjidang developed a distinctive version of feminism from within Neo-Confucianism. Nothing could be more unreasonable and anachronistic than to claim that Yunjidang should have challenged the Neo-Confucian knowledge system itself, which in Yi's view was inherently patriarchal and hierarchical, in order to generate authentic female moral subjectivity.

Unlike Yi Suk-in, Kim Youngmin asks us to take seriously the Neo-Confucian metaphysics of *li*, in which the idea of the political obtains a radically decentered meaning. As Kim sees it, Yunjidang attempted neither to go beyond the inner chambers, as the Enthusiasts claim, nor to shut herself off from social responsibility, as some Skeptics assert. Rather, she was one of the *unremarkable* Neo-Confucian philosophers who, like many of her contemporaries (mostly men), aspired to become a sage through the earnest practice of rituals. For Kim, other than the fact that Yunjidang was a woman, there is nothing noteworthy in her wholehearted embrace of the Neo-Confucian metaphysics of *li* and, as noted, her significance in Korean history (and in the history of Korean Confucianism) lies in the mere fact that she engaged in Confucianism philosophically as a woman. In Kim's view, Yunjidang did not study Confucianism from her distinctive philosophical standpoint as a woman, hence attributing to her merely "performative significance." Two questions are in order.

My first question is whether Yunjidang was indeed "unremarkable" as a female philosopher. Is it fair to say that Yunjidang's significance in the history of Korean philosophy lies in the mere fact that she was a woman philosopher interested in Neo-Confucian ethics and metaphysics? Like Yi Suk-in, Kim does not investigate the further-reaching implications of Yunjidang's own Neo-Confucian account of the particularized embodied nature for the Confucian ethics of moral self-cultivation toward female sagehood; nor does he actively endorse the fact, acknowledged by virtually all contemporary scholars of Yunjidang, that she pursued female sagehood based on moral equality between men and women, a question that captivated no male participants in the Horak debate. Certainly, it would be far-fetched to say that the whole system of Yunjidang's philosophical thought was motivated by her feminist interest in women's moral standing and protection of their moral and material well-being. But it seems equally unreasonable to disregard the feminist aspect of her thought, which became salient in the course of her indirect engagement with the Horak debate and her lifelong quest for female sagehood.

Kim may counter that this does not undermine his argument that Yunjidang can hardly be understood as a feminist because she never attempted to go beyond the inner chambers, considering her active internalization of the norms and virtues cherished within the inner chambers. This brings us to my second question: Did Yunjidang completely reject the value of women's participation in "the public world" as conventionally demarcated from the inner chambers in the Chosŏn society? One question Kim does not seem to address is why it was so important for male Korean Confucians to take part in the public world, where they could freely exchange their philosophical and political ideas, often in writing, and where they could directly involve themselves in public affairs and governance. To be sure, an increasing number of the so-called backwood scholars (k. *sallim* 山林) in the late Chosŏn period chose not to take the civil examination and decided instead to fully immerse themselves in the Learning of the Way (*daoxue* 道學).[131] Indeed, we can make sense of their internal moral reasoning from the perspective of *li*, which justifies a nonpolitical way of exercising one's social responsibility as mandated by the Heavenly Principle.[132] However, this does not mean that Neo-Confucians failed to note the important distinction between serving in the government and serving the Way as a private scholar just as they were clearly aware of the salient moral (hence, not merely functional) demarcation between the outer public world and the inner chambers. If this distinction was not important, as recommended by the Neo-Confucian philosophy of *li*, then why didn't any male Confucian believe that they could attain Confucian sagehood by practicing female virtues?

Contrary to Kim's skepticism, Yunjidang was remarkable precisely in the sense that she turned the Neo-Confucian philosophy of *li* into a principled argument for moral equality between men and women, as well as women's moral capability of attaining sagehood. In eighteenth-century Korea, one of the primary concerns of the Neo-Confucians was whether serving the Way as a private scholar could have equivalent moral significance as serving in the

---

[131] Hein Cho, "The Historical Origin of Civil Society in Korea," *Korea Journal* 37 (1997), pp. 24–41.

[132] For an insightful analysis of the rise of Zhu Xi's Neo-Confucianism as the scholarly and spiritual movement of the Learning of the Way, see Hoyt C. Tillman, *Confucian Discourse and Chu Hsi's Ascendancy* (Honolulu: University of Hawaii Press, 1992).

government, a high goal even for male members from aristocratic backgrounds due, as Kim Youngmin rightly noted, to the shortage of public posts during the late Chosŏn period when there was a steady increase in population. And, undoubtedly, this was, at its core, a male concern, although it must also have been one of the key concerns of mothers of sons. Even if we accept Kim Youngmin's Neo-Confucian philosophical explanation of Yunjidang's inner reasoning, the focus should be not so much on why she did not have to go beyond the inner chambers but how she reinvented the inner chambers into the public world through her creative reinterpretation of Neo-Confucianism, thereby encouraging women to become coparticipants with their male counterparts in the ideal of sagehood.

Yet, there is another point to make regarding Yunjidang's so-called performative significance. Kim Youngmin has failed to recognize that Yunjidang indeed attempted to go beyond the inner chambers in two important ways. First, it is worth mentioning that Yunjidang composed all of her writings in classical Chinese, and only parts of these were initially selected by herself and later included in the *Yunjidang yugo*. This critically differentiates her from other notable female writers of the Chosŏn dynasty, most of whom composed their literary works in vernacular Korean, the main written medium for women and commoners since its invention in the mid-fifteenth century. Thus, she clearly knew that the main audience for her writings would be male members of the *yangban* class versed in Neo-Confucianism as well as some elite women capable of reading classical Chinese, like Kang Chŏngildang several decades later. Given the provocative nature of her philosophical claims, it is not difficult to understand why Yunjidang wanted male Neo-Confucians to read and engage with her writings,[133] while encouraging (elite) women to cultivate themselves to become sages. This is far from being stuck in the inner chambers and diligently practicing female rituals. It was, in essence, an important *public* performance, anticipating her posthumous participation in the broader intellectual world, clearly evidenced by her own selection of the entries to her anthology and having them sent to her younger brother in case the originals in her possession got lost.[134] Indeed, as Yunjidang wished, and contrary to Kim Youngmin's assessment, more than a few male Neo-Confucians after her time spoke highly of her philosophical writings and acknowledged the extraordinary

---

[133] See *Yunjidang yugo* 40a where Yunjidang calls on later scholars to engage with her philosophical interpretations.

[134] According to Im Chŏngju's biography, Yunjidang selected forty items for inclusion in her anthology but the coeditors later created the extant version of the *Yunjidang yugo*, consisting of a total of thirty-five entries, by removing some repetitive items while adding a few new items that Yunjidang produced in her later years.

nature of her scholarship. For them, the crux of Yunjidang's extraordinary performance lay not in the mere fact that she was a woman or a female philosopher but in the superb quality of her philosophical writings. All in all, through this posthumous participation in the otherwise male dominated intellectual world, Yunjidang made a *public* argument that men and women are morally equal and women are equally capable of becoming sages.[135]

Second, and relatedly, the fact that Yunjidang selected the items to be included in her posthumous anthology and asked her brother to publish it shows that she was self-consciously contesting the inner–outer division within the family, an important "public" realm according to Neo-Confucianism, thereby redefining the place of women in it. As Kim Youngmin rightly notes, Yunjidang, like other Neo-Confucians, understood the family as the quintessential public sphere; but unlike male Neo-Confucians, she did not approach the public value of the family purely from an ethical standpoint – namely, as the realm where moral education takes place, especially during the formative stage of one's life, and where one can cultivate virtues that can be extended to other life spheres, including the political arena. She paid extra attention to another public dimension of the family, which was so important for the Neo-Confucians of the *yangban* background: the place that preserves, publishes, and makes widely available the writings of its members so that they can be venerated over generations within the family and beyond. Chosŏn's social convention, however, held that the right to have one's writings preserved, published, and venerated belongs solely to the male members of the family. In the social milieu of eighteenth-century Korea, Yunjidang's initial screening of the items to be included in her posthumous anthology, in anticipation of its eventual publication by her own and her husband's male family members, was an extraordinary *public action*, transgressing conventional ritual boundaries with the effect of repositioning herself (or any female intellectuals for that matter) beyond the inner chambers.

3.3 The Primacy of the Family

My argument thus far has focused on the feminist dimension of both Yunjidang's philosophical thought and her challenges to the prevailing social practices of eighteenth-century Korea. I believe this is sufficient to make Yunjidang a Confucian feminist. Does this mean that the Enthusiasts'

---

[135] For later male Korean Neo-Confucians' appraisals of Yunjidang's philosophical writings, see Kim Kyŏng-mi (김경미), "Chosŏn hugi namsŏng chisiginŭi yŏsŏng chisigine taehan p'yŏngkka (조선 후기 남성 지식인의 여성 지식인에 대한 평가) [The Evaluations of Female Intellectuals by Male Intellectuals in the Late Chosŏn Period]," *Yŏsŏng munhak yŏn'gu* 42 (2017), pp. 35–63.

interpretation of Yunjidang is entirely correct? Skeptics may object, saying that she still falls short of the requirement of stage three for institutional changes to bring about women's equality relative to men. After all, they would argue, Yunjidang seems to have failed to explore new social and political institutions that could ensure and protect equality between men and women. In fact, when the Enthusiasts draw our attention to the far-reaching implications of Yunjidang's argument on moral equality between men and women for educational reform and the equal right to public education, they are certainly geared toward making her a Confucian feminist in the sense of stage three. It is questionable, though, whether Yunjidang's Neo-Confucian philosophy can be read as a subversive political platform as some strong Enthusiasts like Yi Hyechin claim. There is no evidence to suggest that Yunjidang's frustration with the unequal opportunities between men and women in respect of education (i.e., her stage one feminism) further motivated her to justify institutional changes of the sort that would disrupt the existing social and political order – an action comparable to Wollstonecraft's espousal of the political rights of women.

In my view, however, it is deeply problematic to establish simple parallelism between Yunjidang and a modern Western liberal feminist like Wollstonecraft given the radically different intellectual (and political) contexts. In modern Europe, the family was regarded as the private domain marked by the unequal power between parents and children and between husband and wife and it was starkly distinguished from the public domain of political participation and equal citizenship. As Carole Pateman powerfully shows, in modern European political theory and social imaginaries, the family was thought to originate from the "sexual contract," which justified in liberal terms the subjection of women and children to men's unjust domination as husband and father.[136] Unsurprisingly, the single greatest concern of modern Western feminists was to liberate women from their unequal moral and political standing cemented within the family and reinvent them into equal citizens fully equipped with civil and political rights, the most important of which was the right to political participation. Pivoted around the protection of rights and citizenship, therefore, modern liberal feminism naturally entailed a demand for legal changes and political reforms.

Yunjidang's Neo-Confucian world was a total stranger to this rigid demarcation between the family as the private domain and political society as the public domain, which harkens back to the Greek distinction between the *polis* and the *oikos*. As discussed earlier, eighteenth-century Korean Neo-Confucians firmly believed that, from a moral standpoint, the family was coeval with political society (or the state) as the quintessential public realm centrally concerned with

---

[136] Carole Pateman, *The Sexual Contract* (Stanford, CA: Stanford University Press, 1988).

one's moral self-cultivation. As a Neo-Confucian scholar, Yunjidang had no reason to develop her feminist thought in the form of "liberation theory" with a view to emancipating women from the family as the realm of inequality and making them equal members of political society, the only public domain in the Western republican tradition. Moreover, insofar as rights are needed for the purpose of liberating individuals from existing, often oppressive, social conventions as well as helping to empower them to start their lives anew,[137] there was no motivation for Yunjidang to appeal to rights in reconceiving the relationship between men and women and women's moral agency. For what was vitally important for her was whether and how a woman can experience moral growth and become a sage, not how to make women "political agents" as understood in the liberal–republican tradition.

Rather than attempting to liberate women, including herself, from the family, Yunjidang reimagined women's moral dignity primarily within the family by encouraging them to conduct themselves according to the moral principle – *daoli* 道理 as Zhu Xi famously called it – of ritual propriety, which requires reflexive understanding and deliberative application of rituals.[138] She believed that reflexive application of the moral principle of ritual propriety would keep one from blindly adhering to conventional ritual practices. This conviction led her to contest some of the traditional social norms that defined women's ritual roles and regulated their social conduct in violation of their proper intellectual and moral education and their moral worth. I have already discussed how Yunjidang consciously transgressed ritual norms that prevented women from participating in the philosophical world by preparing her own posthumous anthology as well as by chastising Lady Han's father for failing to give her adequate access to education. There are two other cases that show Yunjidang's reflexive reappropriation of the moral principles of righteousness and ritual propriety in the service of a woman's moral agency.

The first case concerns Yunjidang's critical reevaluation of wifely virtues. Since Yunjidang's husband died at the age of twenty-five, only eight years into their marriage, there is little mention of him throughout the *Yunjidang yugo*. Yet, she left two statements after completing her late husband's unfinished

---

[137] Waldron calls this "the fallback theory" of rights. See Jeremy Waldron, "When Justice Replaces Affection: The Need for Rights," *Harvard Journal of Law & Public Policy* 11:3 (1988), pp. 625–647.

[138] In this connection, it is worth noting that Yunjidang stresses the importance of "the expedient" (*quan* 權) in making a moral decision by understanding it as deliberative and practical judgment as required by the given situation; see *Yunjidang yugo* 5a and 23a. See also Philip J. Ivanhoe and Hwa Yeong Wang, "Two Korean Women Confucian Philosophers: Im Yunjidang and Gang Jeongildang," *Journal of Confucian Philosophy and Culture* 36 (2021), pp. 29–53; Kim, "Yunjidang's Feminism and Gender Equality," pp. 156–157.

transcriptions of the *Shijing* (詩經, *The Book of Poetry*), one of the key Confucian classics, and the *Chuci* (楚辭), a collection of literary works by prominent ancient Chinese intellectuals and a must-read for later Confucian scholars as part of their literary training. In deciding to complete her late husband's unfinished transcriptions and hand them down to their posterity, Yunjidang was clearly aware that it would be considered inappropriate for a wife to complete the scholarly work left unfinished by her husband. It would have been a presumptuous thing for a woman to do because for Confucian scholars, transcribing classical texts was an important part of their philological and literary training, essential to their intellectual development. Yunjidang, however, reconceived of a wife's duty in light of the moral principle of ritual propriety, which led her to find a way to fulfill her husband's unrealized scholarly desire, while giving her a chance to immerse herself in classical studies and strengthen her moral agency. Here we find no grand plan to subvert the existing Confucian social order; nor do we see a revolutionary mind that aspires to liberate women from the shackles of Confucian rituals and advance their political rights. What Yunjidang shows us is a firsthand demonstration of how a woman can become dignified within the family through creative reinter-pretation of wifely virtues, which in turn called for a reconfiguring of the moral significance of the family itself, especially for women.

The second case has to do with Yunjidang's critical evaluation of two Korean women, Ch'oe and Hong. According to Yunjidang, a solider whose surname was Hong was murdered but the murderer was not brought to justice. Several years later, his wife (Ch'oe) and daughter (Hong) finally avenged their husband/ father by killing the murderer, then turned themselves in to the authorities. Eventually, they were both acquitted from their criminal charges and further venerated for their virtues of wifely fidelity to the late husband (*lie* 烈) and filial piety (*xiao* 孝), respectively. In the modern sense of criminal justice, the government's veneration of their private vengeance might seem odd because it is likely to undermine the very purpose of establishing a public authority that is supposed to monopolize the power to punish criminals. Indeed, Chosŏn's Confucian state did not tolerate private vengeance, but, at times, it pardoned those who committed a crime with the right moral motives that it publicly promoted, such as filial piety and brotherly love. But, most often, those who were acquitted by the government were men who avenged their family members because, in late Chosŏn, women (widows in particular) were generally expected to continue to fulfill female virtues that were peculiar to their passivity, such as keeping chastity or, in extreme cases, committing suicide. Such social expect-ation was premised on the assumption of the hierarchical relationship between man (husband) and woman (wife).

Yunjidang spoke highly of Ch'oe and Hong for their undaunted exercise of the virtues of fidelity, filial piety, and courage. As Kim Mi-yŏng rightly notes, in the Confucian tradition courage was one of the virtues typically used to describe the character of the *junzi*.[139] In attributing not only fidelity and filial piety but also courage to Ch'oe and Hong, Yunjidang appears to have encouraged women's proactive appropriation of virtues, even ones commonly associated with a man's moral character, as long as doing so was consistent with the moral principle of righteousness, as strongly vindicated by the *Chunqiu* (春秋, *The Spring and Autumn Annals*), a Confucian classic. Thus, what is important in carrying out so-called female virtues is not so much what is conventionally expected of women as passive subjects confined in the inner chambers, but their active moral agency in critically reassessing the given social norms and conventions from the perspective of the moral principles that ought to undergird them. In Yunjidang's view, therefore, there may be virtues that are, in general, better suited to a man's or a woman's Heaven-given nature. But the distinction between male and female virtues, though hardly arbitrary, is not absolute or immutable. It is always subject to the circumstances that require a moral agent's deliberation and particularistic judgment in light of the otherwise universal and unchanging moral principles that are rooted in human nature.

Thus understood, Yunjidang's appraisal of Ch'oe and Hong was not to valorize private vengeance per se, although Confucian classics such as the *Mengzi* (孟子), albeit arguably, endorse a vengeance for parents.[140] What she tried to convey is that there is no distinction between men and women in conducting oneself according to moral principles, even if doing so sometimes involves contesting the heavily gendered moral boundaries set by the male-dominant society. Though Yunjidang did not spell it out, this also has profound implications for moral relationships within the family, between husband and wife and between father and daughter. The belief that women must be guided by moral principles and not by social conventions further entails that the wifely virtue of gentleness is far from submissiveness as stipulated by the "Three Followings for Women." For Yunjidang, marriage was not a sexual contract that legally justifies a man's domination over a woman. Like *yin* and *yang*, as Yunjidang understood them, two equal forces of the moral universe, a husband and a wife should be partners and coparticipants in the way toward moral self-cultivation, and ultimately sagehood.

---

[139] Kim, "Sŏngnihak'esŏ taedudoen kongchŏk yŏngyŏge," pp. 240–241. For an illuminating discussion on the story of Ch'oe and Hong, see also Yi, *Chosŏncho hugi yŏsŏng chisŏngsa*, pp. 108–109.

[140] *Mencius* 7B7.

Likewise, a daughter is no different than a son in terms of her relationship with the father. If a son's vengeance for his father is understood and endorsed as an expression of his filial piety, the same should apply to a daughter and there should be no social prejudice against a woman who has the audacity to fulfill her filial piety by seeking righteous vengeance. By implication, if the relationship between father and son is essentially a moral relationship and a son's filial piety includes not only obedience to the father but also remonstrance toward him when he goes astray from the Way, the same must apply to the relationship between father and daughter. Insofar as a daughter's vengeance for her father is justified not merely for the reason of consanguinity, as some contemporary scholars take the kernel of Confucianism to be,[141] but by the moral principle that underscores filial piety, her expression, too, of the virtue of filial piety must be guided by the same moral standard, which renders filial piety to be a combination of obedience and remonstrance.

For Yunjidang, therefore, the family is a public space because it is regulated by the moral principles of righteousness and ritual propriety. It is by remaking the family in this Neo-Confucian sense that it can gain its public significance for both men and women who are guided by the same moral principles. For liberal feminists, this may hardly signal a necessary institutional change toward protecting the dignity of women. They may also find it difficult to understand Yunjidang's painstaking effort to reformulate the moral significance of the family from the seedbed of Confucian patriarchy into the public realm, thus ensuring moral equality between men and women both through the reconceptualization of female virtues and the empowerment of women's moral agency within the family. However, that Yunjidang was not a liberal feminist does not undermine the fact that she was a feminist of a different sort, a Confucian feminist who believed in moral equality between men and women and reconceived the family as a truly public realm through the creative reappropriation of Neo-Confucianism.

Seen in this way, nothing could be more unreasonable and anachronistic than to expect her to have gone beyond the Neo-Confucian knowledge system in toto like a Platonic philosopher who steps out of "the cave" and sees the light of the truth. Again, Yunjidang never imagined the world outside of ordinary life, nor did she posit the existence of true knowledge that transcends life here and now. In the absence of viable alternative knowledge systems that she could readily avail herself of in order to advance the dignity of women, she wrestled within the Neo-Confucian moral and metaphysical frameworks both to justify moral

---

[141] Qingping Liu, "Filiality versus Sociality and Individuality: On Confucianism as 'Consanguinitism'," *Philosophy East and West* 53 (2003), pp. 234–250.

equality between men and women and to empower women, not as the bearers of rights, but as the possessors of formidable moral character who could conduct themselves according to all-encompassing moral principles.

Summary and Conclusion

Despite the mushrooming of historical, sociological, anthropological, and philosophical studies on women in premodern East Asia, many contemporary scholars still remain puzzled over how to make sense of women's agency in the Confucian context, which they generally understand as androcentric, patriarchal, and unjustly hierarchical. The most common approach among social scientists, in vindicating the moral and social agency of East Asian women, has been to examine how they found a way out of their otherwise agentless Confucian-based social lives and explored alternative lifestyles that enabled them to exercise their authentic and autonomous selfhood. Others who struggle to make sense of women's agency in the Confucian context have drawn attention to women's strategic utilization of Confucian culture in the service of their social agency. I categorized these approaches "external" to women's agency as they do not represent Confucian women's self-understanding of their personhood and moral agency. The external approach informs us about Chinese/ Korean/Japanese women's social agency in the premodern context but it hardly tells us anything about a Confucian woman's moral agency. In this Element, I have employed an "internal approach" to the moral agency of women who had a strong identity as Confucian and who wrestled to establish themselves as female *junzi*. Im Yunjidang presented a perfect case for this study because she was one of the few exceptional women throughout Confucian history who provided a critical reflection on and philosophical investigation of a woman's moral agency in Confucian terms through a sophisticated set of philosophical writings.

In order to understand Yunjidang's philosophical mind, I began with the political and intellectual contexts in which she found herself in eighteenth-century Chosŏn Korea and examined how she indirectly took part in the Horak debate, one of the major philosophical debates among Korean Neo-Confucians during the Chosŏn dynasty, through her lifelong intellectual communication with Im Sŏngju, her brother and mentor. I showed that Yunjidang was particularly immersed in the second and third questions of the Horak debate – whether sages and commoners share the same heart–mind and whether the natures of human beings and nonhuman animals and other things in the moral universe are identical – and answered the second question in the affirmative and the third question in the negative, without siding with either side of the debate.

Special attention was paid to how Yunjidang, in the course of grappling with the second question, was able to advance a novel Neo-Confucian account of (human) nature as a particularized and embodied form with a distinctive endowment of *qi*, leading her to develop two important philosophical claims: (1) from a moral standpoint, human beings share the same nature among themselves regardless of sex; and (2) from a metaphysical standpoint, men and women possess different physical natures, making it suitable (or natural) for each sex to form distinctive moral characteristics that are peculiar to their natural composition decreed by Heaven or the Heavenly Principle.

Then, I showed that Yunjidang's creative reinterpretation of Neo-Confucian metaphysics enabled her to make a radical argument: that men and women are morally equal both in the sense of possessing the same Heaven-given nature with an equal capability of moral self-cultivation, and in terms of the possibility of female sagehood that is morally equal to male sagehood. This raised a question of whether Yunjidang can be understood as a feminist philosopher and, if so, what kind of feminism she proposed, accordingly leading us to turn to the recent debate on Yunjidang as a feminist. I critically examined either side of the debate – the Enthusiasts, on one side, and the Skeptics, on the other – and found the Enthusiasts, notwithstanding their internal disagreements, more agreeable than the Skeptics from the standpoint of what I call a "stage approach" to feminism that rejects a sweeping and West-centric account of feminism that is insensitive to cultural differences.

Although the Enthusiasts often exaggerate Yunjidang's influence on the advancement of women's rights or public education reform, the Skeptics are more at fault in dismissing the progressive and feminist dimension of Yunjidang's philosophical arguments, either by obliterating the important difference between her and the male Korean Neo-Confucians of her time or by assuming Yunjidang's total subscription to the dominant knowledge system of the time, thus making her philosophical ideas indistinguishable and unremarkable. It has been central to my argument that Yunjidang was a remarkable female Neo-Confucian philosopher, not only in the sense of developing critical reflections on and subtle philosophical justifications for Confucian women's moral agency, but also in the sense of offering a penetrating insight into the way in which the Confucian public space could be expanded and made more inclusive without challenging the Neo-Confucian premise of the moral primacy of the family, the quintessential public realm according to Neo-Confucianism.

By way of concluding this Element, I would like to make one additional point. The fact that Yunjidang made a progressive and feminist argument for

moral equality between men and women and for the possibility of female
sagehood does not necessarily make her a modern thinker, unless we revamp
the habit of understanding tradition and modernity in binary terms. Like the
mainstream Neo-Confucians of her time, Yunjidang was strongly associated
with the dominant Yulgok school and as an avid follower of Zhu Xi she was
wholeheartedly committed to "the Great Righteousness of the *Spring and
Autumn*" (*Chunqiu dayi* 春秋大義), which had long undergirded the hierarchical moral relationships between Ming (as the suzerain) and Chosŏn (as the
vassal state), between lord and minister, between father and son, and, by
implication, between husband and wife.[142] Her critical commentaries on well-
known historical figures such as Zhong You (仲由, c. 540–480 BC), Wang Anshi
(王安, 1021–86), and Sima Guang (司馬光, 1019–86) all powerfully demonstrate that her moral appraisal of historical events was hardly distinguishable
from that held by orthodox (male) Neo-Confucians who took part in the Horak
debate. Stated more bluntly, Yunjidang's understanding of Chinese history
reveals remarkable similarity with some of the most conservative Neo-
Confucian intellectuals of the late Chosŏn period who, for instance, vilified
Wang Anshi, best known for his political reform plans during the Northern Song
period, as a petty man, one of the most serious despoilers of the Confucian
Way.[143]

What is remarkable is that Yunjidang, a political conservative, applied the
Great Righteousness of the *Spring and Autumn* to the relationships between
husband and wife and between father and daughter, with the surprising effect
of strengthening women's moral agency. That is, by encouraging women to
conduct themselves not according to social conventions but by the moral
principles of righteousness and ritual propriety that are supposed to underpin
them, Yunjidang stressed the importance of women's capability of moral
deliberation and judgment in their ritual practices. It is curious how
Yunjidang would have come to grips with the seeming tension between her
political conservatism and her progressive feminist philosophy. But it does not
seem to be utterly implausible to believe that she might have seen no critical
tension here because the question of moral equality between men and women
could be thought to be independent of whether some historical figures or
events should be judged as good or bad. Absent Yunjidang's writings

---

[142] For the rise of the idea of the Great Righteousness of the *Spring and Autumn* in seventeenth-
century Korea, see Chi Tu-hwan (지두환), "Ch'ŏng'ŭm kim sanghŏnŭi saeng'ewa sasang:
Ch'unch'u taeŭironŭl chumsimŭro (청음 김상헌의 생애와 사상: 춘추대의론을 중심으로)
[The Life and Thought of Ch'ŏng'ŭm Kim Sang-hŏn: Focusing on His Account of the Great
Righteousness of the *Spring and Autumn*]," *Han'gukhak nonchong* 24 (2001), pp. 65–94.
[143] *Yunjidang yugo* 19b–21b.

containing her full-blown political philosophy, it is difficult to understand to what extent her political philosophy was influenced by her progressive philosophy or whether it contains any feminist element. In any event, there is a danger in presenting Yunjidang as a harbinger of modernity by completely sidelining her subscription to the Neo-Confucian political orthodoxy of eighteenth-century Korea.

References

Ackerly, B. A. "Is Liberalism the Only Way toward Democracy? Confucianism and Democracy," *Political Theory*, 33(2005), 547–576.

Adler, J. A. *Reconstructing the Confucian Dao: Zhu Xi's Appropriation of Zhou Dunyi* (Albany: State University of New York Press, 2014).

Angle, S. C. *Sagehood: The Contemporary Significance of Neo-Confucian Philosophy* (New York: Oxford University Press, 2009).

Angle, S. C. *Contemporary Confucian Political Philosophy* (Cambridge: Polity, 2012).

Angle, S. C. and Tiwald, J. *Neo-Confucianism: A Philosophical Introduction* (Cambridge: Polity, 2017).

Arendt, H. *The Human Condition* (Chicago, IL: University of Chicago Press, 1958).

Bloom, I. "Mencian Confucianism and Human Rights" in W. T. de Bary and W. Tu (eds.), *Confucianism and Human Rights* (New York: Columbia University Press, 1998), pp. 94–116.

Brooks, E. B. and Brooks, A. T. *The Original Analects: Sayings of Confucius and His Successors* (New York: Columbia University Press, 1998).

Chan, W.-T. "The Evolution of the Confucian Concept of *Jen*," *Philosophy East and West*, 4(1955), 295–319.

Chi, T.-H. (지두환) "Ch'ŏng'ŭm kim sanghŏnŭi saeng'ewa sasang: Ch'unch'u taeŭironŭl chumsimŭro (청음 김상헌의 생애와 사상: 춘추대의론을 중심 으로) [The Life and Thought of Ch'ŏng'ŭm Kim Sang-hŏn: Focusing on His Account of the Great Righteousness of the *Spring and Autumn*]," *Han'gukhak nonchong*, 24(2001), 65–94.

Cho, H. "The Historical Origin of Civil Society in Korea," *Korea Journal*, 37 (1997), 24–41.

Cho, S.-S. (조성산) "18segi horak nonjaenggwa noron sasanggyeŭi punhwa 18 (세기 호락논쟁과 노론 사상계의 분화) [The Horak Debate during the Eighteenth Century and the Differentiation within the Dominant Faction of the Yulgok School]," *Han'guk sasangsa hak*, 8 (1997), 75–111.

Chŏng, S.-W. (정순우) *Sŏdangŭi sahoesa* (서당의 사회사) [*The Sociology of the Local Private Village School*] (Seoul: T'aehaksa, 2012).

Chow, K.-W. *The Rise of Confucian Ritualism in Late Imperial China* (Stanford, CA: Stanford University Press, 1994).

Chu, H. *Learning to Be a Sage*, trans. D. K. Gardner (Berkeley: University of California Press, 1990).

Chung, E. Y. J. *The Korean Neo-Confucianism of Yi T'oegye and Yi Yulgok: A Reappraisal of the "Four-Seven Thesis" and Its Practical Implications for Self-Cultivation* (Albany: State University of New York Press, 1995).

Confucius, *The Analects*, trans. D. C. Lau (New York: Penguin, 1979).

Creel, H. G. *Confucius and the Chinese Way* (New York: Harper & Row, 1949).

De Bary, W. T. *The Liberal Tradition in China* (New York: Columbia University Press, 1983).

Deuchler, M. *The Confucian Transformation of Korea: A Study of State and Ideology* (Cambridge, MA: Council on East Asian Studies, Harvard University, 1992).

Deuchler, M. "Despoilers of the Way – Insulters of the Sages: Controversies over the Classics in Seventeenth-Century Korea" in J. K. Haboush and M. Deuchler (eds.), *Culture and the State in Late Chosŏn Korea* (Cambridge, MA: Harvard University Asia Center, 1999), pp. 91–133.

Deuchler, M. "Propagating Female Virtues in Chosŏn Korea" in D. Ko, J. K. Haboush, and J. R. Piggott (eds.), *Women and Confucian Cultures in Premondern China, Korea, and Japan* (Berkeley: University of California Press, 2003), pp. 142–169.

Ebrey, P. B. *The Inner Quarters: Marriage and the Lives of Chinese Women in the Sung Period* (Berkeley: University of California Press, 1993).

Elman, B. A. *Civil Examinations and Meritocracy in Late Imperial China* (Cambridge, MA: Harvard University Press, 2013).

Eno, R. *The Confucian Creation of Heaven: Philosophy and the Defense of Ritual Mastery* (Albany: State University of New York Press, 1990).

Fetzer, J. and Soper, J. C. *Confucianism, Democratization, and Human Rights in Taiwan* (Lanham, MD: Lexington Books, 2013).

Gardner, D. K. *Chu Hsi: Learning to Be a Sage* (Berkeley: University of California Press, 1990).

Goldin, P. R. "The View of Women in Early Confucianism" in C. Li (ed.), *The Sage and the Second Sex* (Chicago, IL: Open Court, 2000), pp. 139–143.

Haboush, J. K. "Constructing the Center: The Ritual Controversy and the Search for a New Identity in Seventeenth-Century Korea" in J. K. Haboush and M. Deuchler (eds.), *Culture and the State in Late Chosŏn Korea* (Cambridge, MA: Harvard University Asia Center, 1999), pp. 46–90.

Hahm, C. "Ritual and Constitutionalism: Disputing the Ruler's Legitimacy in a Confucian Polity," *American Journal of Comparative Law*, 57(2009), 135–204.

Helgesen, G. *Democracy and Authority in Korea: The Cultural Dimension in Korean Politics* (Richmond, UK: Curzon, 1998).

Hong, J.-G. (홍정근) "Is the Morality of Human Beings Superior to the Morality of Non-Human Beings? Debate over Human versus Animal Nature in the Joseon Period," *Korea Journal*, 51(2011), 72–96.

Huntington, S. P. *The Third Wave: Democratization in the Late Twentieth Century* (Norman: University of Oklahoma Press, 1991).

Im, S. (임성주) *Nongmunjip* (鹿門集) [*The Collected Writings of Im Sŏngju*]. https://db.itkc.or.kr/dir/item?itemId=MO#dir/node?grpId=&itemId=MO&gubun=book&depth=2&cate1=Z&cate2=&dataGubun=%EC%84%9C%EC%A7%80&dataId=ITKC_MO_0532A.

Im, Y. (임윤지당) *Yunjidang yugo* (允摯堂遺稿) [*The Bequeathed Writings of Im Yunjidang*]. https://db.itkc.or.kr/dir/item?itemId=MO#/dir/node?dataId=ITKC_MO_1072A.

Ivanhoe, P. J. "Metaphysics, Epistemology, and Ethics" in P. J. Ivanhoe (ed.), *Zhu Xi: Selected Writings* (New York: Oxford University Press, 2019), pp. 14–34.

Ivanhoe, P. J. and Wang, H. Y. "Two Korean Women Confucian Philosophers: Im Yunjidang and Gang Jeongildang," *Journal of Confucian Philosophy and Culture*, 36(2021), 29–53.

Kang, C. (강정일당) *Chŏngildang yugo* (靜一堂遺稿) [*The Bequeathed Writings of Kang Chŏngildang*]. https://db.itkc.or.kr/dir/item?itemId=MO#dir/node?grpId=&itemId=MO&gubun=book&depth=2&cate1=Z&cate2=&dataGubun=%EC%84%9C%EC%A7%80&dataId=ITKC_MO_1163A.

Kang, N.-S. (강남순) "Yugyowa p'eminisŭm: Kŭ pulganŭnghan manname taehayŏ (유교와 페미니즘: 그 불가능한 만남에 대하여) [Confucianism and Feminism: On Their Impossible Rendezvous]" in Han'guk yugyo hakhoe (한국유교학회) (ed.), *Yugyuwa p'eminisŭm* (유교와 페미니즘) [*Confucianism and Feminism*] (Seoul: Ch'ŏrakkwa hyŏnsilsa, 2001), pp. 271–282.

Kim, C.-I. (김재임) "Yunjidang yugoe nat'anan yŏsŏng ŭisik koch'al (윤지당 유고에 나타난 여성의식 고찰) [An Examination on the Feminist Consciousness in the *Bequeathed Writings of Im Yunjidang*]," *Hanmun kojŏn yŏn'gu*, 10(2005), 215–256.

Kim, C.-I. "Im yunjidangŭi songnironŭl t'onghae pon in'ganhak kujo (임윤지당의 성리론을 통해 본 인간학 구조) [Im Yunjidang's Neo-Confucian Philosophy of Human Nature and the Structure of Her Philosophical Understanding of Human Being]," *Kangwŏn munhwa yŏn'gu* 26(2007), 173–188.

Kim, H. (김현) "Sŏngnihakchŏk kach'igwanŭi hwaksan'gwa yŏsŏng (성리학적 가치관의 확산과 여성) [The Spread of Neo-Confucian Values and Women]," *Minjok munhwa yŏn'gu*, 41(2004), 455–488.

Kim, H.-C. (김형찬) *Korean Confucianism: The Philosophy and Politics of T'oegye and Yulgok* (London: Rowman & Littlefield International, 2018).

Kim, H.-K. "Yunjidang's Feminism and Gender Equality," *Asian Philosophy*, 31(2021), 143–159.

Kim, H.-S. (김혜숙) "Toward Critical Confucianism: Woman as a Method," *Han'guk yŏsŏng ch'ŏrak*, 26(2016), 131–152.

Kim, K.-M. (김경미) "Chosŏn hugi namsŏng chisiginŭi yŏsŏng chisigine taehan p'yŏngkka (조선 후기 남성 지식인의 여성 지식인에 대한 평가) [The Evaluations of Female Intellectuals by Male Intellectuals in the Late Chosŏn Period]," *Yŏsŏng munhak yŏn'gu*, 42(2017), 35–63.

Kim, K.-M. *Im yunjidang p'yŏngjŏn* (임윤지당 평전) [*A Critical Biography of Im Yunjidang*] (Seoul: Han'gyŏrye ch'ulp'an, 2019).

Kim, M.-Y. (김미영) "Sŏngnihak'esŏ taedudoen kongchŏk yŏngyŏge taehan yŏsŏngjuŭijŏk chŏpkkŭn 성리학에서 대두된 '공적영역'에 대한 여성주의적 접근[A Feminist Approach to the Question of 'Public Sphere' in the Cheng-Zhu Neo-Confucian Context]," *Ch'ŏrak yŏn'gu*, 29(2005), 389–416.

Kim, R. "Human Nature and Animal Nature: The Horak Debate and Its Philosophical Significance" in Y. Back and P. J. Ivanhoe (eds.), *Traditional Korean Philosophy: Problems and Debates* (London: Rowman & Littlefield International, 2017), pp. 85–109.

Kim, S. *Confucian Democracy in East Asia: Theory and Practice* (New York: Cambridge University Press, 2014).

Kim, S. "The Way to Become a Female Sage: Im Yunjidang's Confucian Feminism," *Journal of the History of Ideas*, 75(2014), 395–416.

Kim, S. "From Wife to Moral Teacher: Kang Chŏngildang on Neo-Confucian Self-Cultivation," *Asian Philosophy*, 24(2014), 28–47.

Kim, S. "Making Peace with the Barbarians: Neo-Confucianism and the Pro-Peace Argument in 17th-Century Korea," *European Journal of Political Theory* (November 2020). https://doi.org/10.1177/1474885120963966

Kim, S. "Between Coherence and Principle: *Li* 理 and the Politics of Neo-Confucianism in Late Koryŏ Korea," *Philosophy East and West*, 71(2021), 369–392.

Kim, S. (김세서리아) "Chosŏn sŏngnihagŭi t'aegŭk ŭmyangnonŭl t'onghae pon han'gukchŏk yŏsŏng chuch'e hyŏngsŏng iron mosaek (조선 성리학의 태극음양론을 통해 본 한국적 여성주체형성 이론 모색) [A Search for the Theory of Korean Female Subjectivity Formation through the Discourses of the Great Ultimate and *Yin-Yang*]," *Yuhak yŏn'gu*, 36 (2016), 295–315.

Kim, S. (김세서리아) "Im yunjidangŭi nonŏ ihae'e taehan yŏsŏng ch'ŏrakchŏk sŏngch'al (임윤지당의 논어 이해에 대한 여성철학적 성찰) [A Feminist Reflection on Im Yunjidang's Interpretation of the *Analects*]," *Han'guk yŏsŏng ch'ŏrak*, 28(2017), 27–53.

Kim, Y. "Neo-Confucianism as Free-Floating Resource: Im Yunjidang and Kang Chŏngildang as Two Female Neo-Confucian Philosophers in Late Chosŏn' in Y. Kim and M. J. Pettid (eds.), *Women and Confucianism in Chosŏn Korea: New Perspectives* (Albany: State University of New York Press, 2011), pp. 71–88.

Kim, Y.-.S. (김영수) *Kŏn'gugŭi chŏngch'i: Yŏmal sŏnch'o, hyŏngmyŏnggwa munmyŏng chŏnhwan* (건국의 정치: 여말선초, 혁명과 문명전환) [*The Politics of Founding: Revolution and the Transition of Civilization during the Late Koryŏ and Early Chosŏn Periods*] (Seoul: Ihaksa, 2006).

Ko, D. *Teachers of the Inner Chambers: Women and Culture in Seventeenth Century China* (Stanford, CA: Stanford University Press, 1994).

Ku, M.-C. (구민정) "Im yunjidangŭi chagi chŏngch'esŏngŭi kusŏnge taehayŏ (임윤지당의 자기 정체성의 구성에 대하여) [On the Construction of Im Yunjidang's Self-Identity]," *Inmunhak yŏn'gu*, 29(2019), 27–49.

Lee, C.-S. (이천승) "Philosophical Implications of the Discussion of *Mibal* in the Horak Debate of the Late Joseon Period," *Korea Journal*, 51(2011), 97–117.

Lee, H.-I. (이해임) "Im Yunjidang's View of Material Composition," *Journal of Confucian Philosophy and Culture*, 34(2020), 105–128.

Lee, K.-K. (이경구) "The Horak Debate from the Reign of King Sukjong to King Sunjo," *Korea Journal*, 51(2011), 15–41.

Lee, S.-H. "The Concept of *Gong* in Traditional Korea and Its Modern Transformations," *Korea Journal*, 43(2003), 137–163.

Lee, J. "Zhu Xi's Metaphysical Theory of Human Nature" in K. C. Ng and Y. Huang (eds.), *Dao Companion to Zhu Xi's Philosophy* (Dordrecht: Springer, 2020), pp. 265–287.

Lee P. C. "Li Zhi and John Stuart Mill: A Confucian Feminist Critique of Liberal Feminism' in C. Li (ed.), *The Sage and the Second Sex* (Chicago, IL: Open Court, 2000), pp. 113–132.

Lee. S.-G. (이순구) "Chosŏnsidae kajok chedoŭi pyŏnhwawa yŏsŏng (조선시대 가족제도의 변화와 여성) [The Change of the Family Structure and Women during the Chosŏn Period]," *Yŏsŏng kojŏn munhak yŏn'gu*, 10 (2005), 119–142.

Lee, S.-G. "The Exemplar Wife: The Life of Lady Chang of Andong in Historical Context" in Y. Kim and M. J. Pettid (eds.), *Women and*

Confucianism in Chosŏn Korea: New Perspectives (Albany: State University of New York Press, 2011), pp. 29–48.

Leung, Y.-H. "Zhu Xi and the Debate between Virtue Ethicists and Situationists: Virtue Cultivation as a Possible, Practical, and Necessary Enterprise" in K.-C. Ng and Y. Huang (eds.), *Dao Companion to Zhu Xi's Philosophy* (Dordrecht: Springer, 2020), pp. 895–927.

Liu, Q. "Filiality versus Sociality and Individuality: On Confucianism as 'Consanguinitism'," *Philosophy East and West*, 53(2003), 234–250.

Mencius. *Mencius*, trans. D. C. Lau (New York: Penguin, 1970).

Mun, C.-Y. (문지영) "Yŏsŏng ch'abyŏre taehan tong sŏyangŭi insikkwa tojŏn: Im yunjidanggwa ulstonkraeptŭrŭl chungsimŭro ('여성차별'에 대한 동서양의 인식과 도전: 임윤지당과 울스터크래프트를 중심으로) [The Understanding of and Challenge to 'Discrimination against Women' in East and West: Focusing on Im Yunjidang and Wollstonecraft]," *Han'guk chŏngch'ihak hoebo*, 50(2016), 23–49.

Mun, S.-Y. (문석윤) *Horak nonjaeng hyŏngsŏnggwa chŏn'gae* (호락논쟁 형성과 전개) [*The Origin and Unfolding of the Horak Debate*] (Seoul: Tonggwa sŏ, 2006).

Ni, P. "Seek and You Will Find It; Let Go and You Will Lose It: Exploring a Confucian Approach to Human Dignity," *Dao*, 13(2014), 174–198.

Pae, W.-S. (배우성) *Chosŏn'gwa chunghwa* (조선과 중화) [*Chosŏn and the Sincocentric Civilization*] (Seoul: Tolbegae, 2014).

Pak, H.-S. (박현숙) "Im yunjidangnon (임윤지당론) [A Study on Im Yunjidang]," *Yŏsŏng munhak yŏn'gu*, 9(2003), 131–156.

Pak, H.-S. "Kang chŏngildang: Sŏngnihakchŏk namnyŏ p'yŏngdŭngjuŭija (강정일당: 성리학적 남녀평등주의자) [Kang Chŏngildang: A Neo-Confucian feminist]," *Yŏsŏngmunhak yŏn'gu*, 11(2004), 57–79.

Pateman, C. *The Sexual Contract* (Stanford, CA: Stanford University Press, 1988).

Peterson, M. A. *Korean Adoption and Inheritance: Case Studies in the Creation of Classic Confucian Society* (Ithaca, NY: Cornell University Press, 1996).

Raphals, L. A. "Gendered Virtue Reconsidered: Notes from the Warring States and Han" in C. Li (ed.), *The Sage and the Second Sex* (Chicago, IL: Open Court, 2000), pp. 225–226.

Raphals, L. A. "A Woman Who Understood Rites" in B. W. Van Norden (ed.), *Confucius and the* Analects (New York: Oxford University Press, 2002), pp. 275–302.

Schwartz, B. I. *The World of Thought in Ancient China* (Cambridge, MA: Belknap, 1985).

Son, H.-C. (손흥철) *Nongmun im sŏngjuŭi sam'gwa ch'ŏrak* (녹문 임성주의 삶과 철학) [*The Life and Philosophy of Im Sŏngju*] (Seoul: Chisik sanŏpsa, 2004).

Tan, S.-H. *Confucian Democracy: A Deweyan Reconstruction* (Albany: State University of New York Press, 2004).

Tillman, H. C. *Utilitarian Confucianism: Ch'en Liang's Challenge to Chu Hsi* (Cambridge, MA: Council on East Asian Studies, Harvard University, 1982).

Tillman, H. C. *Confucian Discourse and Chu Hsi's Ascendancy* (Honolulu: University of Hawaii Press, 1992).

Virág, C. "Moral Psychology and Cultivating the Self" in P. J. Ivanhoe (ed.), *Zhu Xi: Selected Writings* (New York: Oxford University Press, 2019), pp. 35–55.

Waldron, J. "When Justice Replaces Affection: The Need for Rights," *Harvard Journal of Law & Public Policy*, 11(1988), 625–647.

Wang, R. R. "Dong Zhongshu's Transformation of '*Yin-Yang*' Theory and Contesting of Gender Identity," *Philosophy East and West*, 55(2005), 209–231.

Wu, K.-S. (우경섭) *Chosŏnjunghwajuŭiŭi sŏnginpgwa tongasia* (조선중화주의의 성립과 동아시아) [*The Formation of Chosŏn Cultural-Centrism and East Asia*] (Seoul: Unistori, 2013).

Yi, H.-C. (이해진) "Yŏsŏng'esŏ 'in'ganŭro, chuch'erŭl hyanghan yŏlmang: Im yunjidang'gwa ulstonkraeptŭ pigyo yŏn'gu ('여성'에서 '인간'으로, 주체를 향한 열망: 임윤지당과 울스턴크래프트 비교 연구) [From Woman to Human, the Passion toward a Moral Subject: A Comparative Study on Im Yunjidang and Wollstonecraft]," *Han'guk yŏsŏnghak*, 30(2014), 89–125.

Yi, H.-S. (이혜순) "Kang chŏnildangŭi ye tamnon (강정일당의 예 담론) [Kang Chŏngidang's Discourse of Rituals]," *Ŏmun yŏn'gu*, 33(2005), 135–159.

Yi, H.-S. (이혜순) *Chosŏncho hugi yŏsŏng chisŏngsa* (조선조 후기 여성 지성사) [*The History of Women Intellectuals in Late Chosŏn*] (Seoul: Ihwa yŏja taehakkyo ch'ulp'anbu, 2007).

Yi, S.-I. "Chosŏnsidae yŏsŏng chisigŭi sŏngkkyŏkkwa kŭ kusŏng wŏlli (조선시대 여성 지식의 성격과 그 구성원리) [The Nature of Women's Knowledge and Its Constitutive Principle during the Chosŏn Period]," *Tongyang ch'ŏrak*, 33(2005), 77–104.

Yi, Ŭ.-S. (이은선) *Irŏbŏrin ch'owŏrŭl ch'ajasŏ: Han'guk yugyoŭi chonggyojŏk sŏngch'algwa yŏsŏngjuŭi* (잃어버린 초월을 찾아서: 한국 유교의 종교적 성찰과 여성주의) [*In Search of Lost Transcendence: Religious Reflexivity and Feminism in Korean Confucianism*] (Seoul: Monsinŭn saramdŭl, 2009).

Yi, W.-C. (이완재) "Songnihagŭi maengnak'esŏ pon ch'ogi kaehw asasang (성리학의 맥락에서 본 초기개화사상) [Early Enlightenment Thought from the Standpoint of Cheng-Zhu Neo-Confucian Philosophy]," *Tongasia muhwa yŏn'gu*, 29(1996), 127–157.

Yi, Y.-C. (이영춘) *Im Yunjidang: Kugyŏk yunjidangyugo* (임윤지당: 국역 윤지당유교) [*Im Yunjidang: A Korean Translation of the Bequeathed Writings of Yunjidang*] (Seoul: Hyean, 1998).

Yu, Y.-H. (유영희) "Im yunjidangŭi sŏngni ch'ŏrakkwa suhaengnon (임윤지당의 성리 철학과 수행론) [Im Yunjidang's Neo-Confucian Philosophy and Her Account of Moral Self-Cultivation]," *Han'guk sasanggwa munhwa*, 29 (2005), 231–261.

Acknowledgments

The author is grateful to two anonymous reviewers for their valuable comments. The research for this Element was supported by a research grant provided by the City university of Hong Kong (CItyU 9610464).

Women in the History of Philosophy

Jacqueline Broad

Monash University

Jacqueline Broad is Associate Professor of Philosophy at Monash University, Australia. Her area of expertise is early modern philosophy, with a special focus on seventeenth and eighteenth-century women philosophers. She is the author of *Women Philosophers of the Seventeenth Century* (CUP, 2002), *A History of Women's Political Thought in Europe, 1400–1700* (with Karen Green; CUP, 2009), and *The Philosophy of Mary Astell: An Early Modern Theory of Virtue* (OUP, 2015).

Advisory Board

About the Series

In this Cambridge Elements series, distinguished authors provide concise and structured introductions to a comprehensive range of prominent and lesser-known figures in the history of women's philosophical endeavour, from ancient times to the present day.

Cambridge Elements ☰

Women in the History of Philosophy

Elements in the Series

Pythagorean Women
Caterina Pellò

Frances Power Cobbe
Alison Stone

Olympe de Gouges
Sandrine Bergès

Simone de Beauvoir
Karen Green

Im Yunjidang
Sungmoon Kim

A full series listing is available at: www.cambridge.org/EWHP

Printed in the USA
CPSIA information can be obtained
at www.ICGtesting.com
LVHW080612120124
768743LV00006B/303